GOD'S OWN KITCHEN

The inspiring story of Akshaya Patra —
a social enterprise run by monks and CEOs

Providing mid-day meals to 1.6 million schoolchildren every day

D1492812

westland ltd

61, II Floor, Silverline Building, Alapakkam Main Road, Maduravoyal, Chennai 600095

93, I Floor, Sham Lal Road, Daryaganj, New Delhi 110002

First published by westland ltd 2017

10 9 8 7 6 5 4 3 2 1

ISBN: 978-93-85724-84-8
Design by Haitenlo Semy

All photos used in this book with the permission of Akshaya Patra Foundation
Photo of the Golden Temple on Page 94-95 © Nivedita Bansal

Printed at Manipal Technologies Ltd, Manipal

Disclaimer

Dedicated to

My dear friend Aneeta

For being an akshaya patra
With open heart and open home

AUTHOR'S NOTE

My first visit to an ISKCON temple was when I was eight years old, in Los Angeles. I remember my father buying a thick book with a colourful illustration on the cover. One of the many written by A C Bhaktivedanta Srila Prabhupada.

But more than that, I remember there was *prasadam*, perhaps a *laddoo*. In fact, my brain automatically associates ISKCON with 'food'. And blessings.

For, every year, I receive a small packet of *kaju* and *kishmish* — exactly on my birthday. Thanks to a very small donation made at ISKCON some 20 years ago.

This association was further strengthened when I first met Madhu Pandit Prabhu in ISKCON Bangalore in December, 2010. I had heard about their mid-day meal program and wanted to know more.

Subsequently, I wrote a chapter on the Akshaya Patra Foundation in my book 'I Have a Dream', which was about social entrepreneurs.

The real 'aha' moment was when I visited Akshaya Patra's Hubli kitchen. It was an amazing amalgamation of technology and true dedication to a cause. To feed 1 lakh children a piping hot, nutritious meal — every day, day after day — is something to be seen, to be admired and learnt from.

And so, I embarked on this journey of writing a book. My instinct is always to tell the story — of the people their minds, their motivations, the many problems they faced.

What I learnt is that no task one undertakes — no matter how noble — is without obstacles.

That obstacles can be overcome, when the mind is clear and the heart has faith.

What we have today is a crisis of faith. No faith in the government, or in institutions, no faith in ourselves.

We offer bribes even to God — 'Here, take this rupee-note, grant my wish!'

Rarely do we feel thankful, or filled with abundance. Little realising what it really is — to 'not have'. To not have a good breakfast before school, or mummy ka tiffin for lunch. Let alone the means to order from Zomato or glug coffee in Starbucks.

Writing this book opened my eyes to what hunger *feels* like. It is horrible and unacceptable and inhumane.

Let us open our hearts, our minds and our wallets to eradicate hunger from this country. Students and CEOs, swamis and socialites — we can do this together.

Love is limitless and it is the key. Be generous, be kind, be happy, be free.

ACKNOWLEDGMENTS

My heartfelt gratitude, affection and regard to Niyati Patel for standing beside me like a rock through the 21-month journey of writing this book. The research took us from Baran to Bhubaneshwar and generated voluminous transcriptions.

Together, we sifted through and made sense of the material. Fact-checked. Double-checked. Wrote and rewrote. Until we were fully and completely satisfied.

This journey would not have been possible without the support of so many within Akshaya Patra, who gladly and freely shared their experiences. In particular, Shridhar Venkat, who was always just a phone call away.

Chanchalapathi Dasa, for not only sharing with me this story. But the essence of the *Bhagavad Gita*.

Thank you to Usha Gururaj for help in liaison and co-ordination.

To Bharati Ghanshyam for initiating this project.

Thank you to the team at Westland — Gautam Padmanabhan, Deepthi Talwar, Karthik Venkatesh, Krishnakumar, Satish Sundaram, Jayanthi & team. For everything.

To Kanick Raj, for his fantastic cover concept and photography. Haitenlo Semy for the clean and crisp layout of this book.

To all the dedicated souls who did the transcription of interviews. And Sheetal Shinde, for organising and spiral-binding them!

My friend Ravish Kumar for reading the draft and providing valuable feedback.

To my mentor and guide Sunil Handa for constantly reminding me — 'Focus!'

To my parents, to Yatin, dear Nivedita, and my life-line, Lata.

To Maya — who reminds me that love comes in many different forms; this one has four legs.

And finally, Divine Intervention in the form of a fracture. A blessing in disguise, for it forced me to put all else aside and sit in one place. Writing, writing and only writing.

Hare Krishna.

CAST OF CHARACTERS

Founders: The spiritualists and capitalists who came together for a cause.

1. Madhu Pandit Dasa: President, ISKCON Bangalore
2. Mohandas Pai: then CFO of Infosys
3. Chanchalapathi Dasa: Vice-President, ISKCON Bangalore
4. Abhay Jain: businessman and childhood friend of Pai

Trustees: The socially-minded professionals who joined the Akshaya Patra board.

1. Ramadas Kamath: Mohan's trusted colleague from Infosys
2. Raj Kondur: Harvard Business School graduate, venture capitalist
3. V Balakrishnan: then VP, Finance – Infosys
4. Desh Deshpande: serial entrepreneur from Boston, USA
5. Ravindra Chamaria: IT infrastructure developer from Kolkata

The A Team: The monks who started the first Akshaya Patra kitchen in Bangalore.

1. Venu Vadana Dasa: operations, logistics
2. Vikram Krishna: design, strategy
3. Chitranga Chaitanya Dasa: program management

Start Up Kitchen Crew: The monks who set up new kitchens across India.

1. Vyompada Dasa & Suvyakta Narasimha Dasa: Vrindavan
2. Ratnangada Govinda Dasa: Jaipur & Baran
3. Yuddhisthira Krishna Dasa & Rajiv Lochana Dasa: Bellary & Hubli
4. Achyutha Krishna Dasa & Panchratna Dasa: Puri, Bhubaneswar, Nayagarh & Rourkela
5. Jaganmohan Dasa: Ahmedabad, Vadodara & Surat
6. Janardhana Dasa: Bhilai & Guwahati
7. Vamshidhara Dasa & Mahavishnu Dasa: Vijayawada

The Professionals: The team who took the organisation to the next level.

1. Shridhar Venkat: Akshaya Patra's first CEO
2. T S Ramaswamy: Head of Finance
3. Rama Prakash: first professional marketing manager
4. Madhu Sridhar: first CEO of Akshaya Patra USA
5. Muralidhar Pundla: GM (process excellence)
6. Dipika Khaitan: Executive Director, Akshaya Patra UK
7. R Madan: joined as COO

Innovators: They were ever ready to solve a new problem.

1. Prahaladisha Dasa: the monk who made the chapati machine
2. Vidya Sagar: the SME guy who did the impossible
3. Ajay Kavishwar: jugaad method of marketing
4. Saanil Bhaskaran: from consultant to call centre guru
5. Vinay Kumar: a CA who is now heading four kitchens

Well-Wishers: They believed in Akshaya Patra, and helped it grow.

1. Sudha Murty: Chairperson, Infosys Foundation
2. Narayana Murthy: Founder, Infosys
3. Dr A P J Abdul Kalam: then President of India
4. Bill Clinton: former President of USA
5. Sudheendra Kulkarni: close aide to former PM, Atal Bihari Vajpayee
6. Prabhakar Kalavacherla: Partner at KPMG
7. B Swarup: a CBDT member and advisor to Akshaya Patra
10. Ravi Narayan: IT professional and an ISKCON devotee

Public leaders who supported Akshaya Patra

1. Dr Murli Manohar Joshi: then Union Minister for Human Resource Development
2. Vasundhara Raje: CM of Rajasthan
3. S M Krishna: former CM of Karnataka
4. Narendra Modi: Prime Minister of India, then CM of Gujarat
5. Naveen Patnaik: CM of Orissa
6. Y S Rajashekhar Reddy: former CM of Andhra Pradesh
7. Raman Singh: CM of Chhattisgarh

PROLOGUE

24th April, 2015

Shridhar Venkat nervously drummed his fingers on the table. Another five minutes and the meeting would begin.

He went over the key points of the presentation in his head. The team had done its job well — all targets had been achieved. In fact, surpassed. But the board members were never easy to please.

As always, the CEO would have to answer some tough questions.

"They are ready for you!" came the message.

Shridhar ascended the stairs and pushed open a heavy wooden door. Seated around a large mahogany table in business-like fashion were 12 expectant men, laptops and tablets in front of them, with Bluetooth devices perched over their ears.

"Aah, the Akshaya Patra team is here. You have an hour for your presentation. Please try not to overshoot it."

Shridhar glanced at the 'busy executives' in the room and could not help smiling. He was used to it, but to anyone else, what a strange sight this would be!

There were no suits and ties to be seen, just flowing orange and white robes. Sandalwood paste *tilaks* on every forehead. And shining, bald heads.

Indeed, these were monks of the ISKCON order. But like their Lord God Krishna, they had taken a different avatar.

Here, at the 16th annual Management Council Meeting of the Akshaya Patra foundation, they were experts in finance and marketing, operations and logistics. Demanding results from their CEO and his crack team of professionals.

For this was the Akshaya Patra Foundation. Its stakeholders — 1.6 million schoolchildren.

Its mission — that no child should go hungry. Its story — an example and inspiration.

The world of matter and the world of spirit are not separate. They work in tandem.

What the soul feels, the mind desires. What the mind desires, the body undertakes.

"Let not the fruits of action be your motive, nor let your attachment be to inaction."

May you live a life of peace, bringing peace unto others.

He who is the Cause of all Causes is watching over you, always.

BHAKTI YOGA

The power of passion and
devotion to a cause
(2000 – 2004)

CHAPTER 1

AARAMBH

August 1999

At 4 o'clock, in the morning, while the city of Bangalore lay asleep, the temple on Hare Krishna Hill stirred to life.

A young man in orange robes and sandalwood tilak blew the conch-shell at the close of the *mangalaarti* — the very first worship ceremony of the day.

Madhu Pandit Dasa felt a sense of peace in the midst of the chanting and clanging of bells. This was that special moment when he felt directly connected to the Lord.

People often asked him — "Why did you leave IIT to become a monk?"

Had he followed the conventional path, Madhu Pandit would have been a big-shot in some large corporation. Instead, he was the 'CEO' of a large temple.

Fundraising, outreach, manpower and maintenance — managing the 7-acre temple campus was a complicated affair.

And these were just the temporal tasks on his plate.

More important was spiritual growth and development — of the Self and of the devotees who had become full-time 'volunteers'. These were highly educated young men — mostly BTechs — attracted to the philosophy of ISKCON (the International Society for Krishna Consciousness).

The path is not easy. It is the path of *nishkama karma* — or selfless action.

When Madhu Pandit first joined ISKCON, he walked on dusty roads from village to village giving Gita *gyan*. Eating only what was given to him as alms, and sleeping wherever he found a place to rest.

In the early '80s, Madhu Pandit settled in Bangalore. Living in a nondescript three-bedroom house with eight other devotees. That was ISKCON Bangalore — a modest organisation — little known to the people of the city.

But in his mind's eye, Madhu Pandit could see something much bigger. A modern temple and cultural complex where people could congregate. Where the wisdom of the *Gita* could flow. Where love for Krishna would grow.

Madhu Pandit convinced the Bangalore Development Authority to allot a piece of land for the proposed temple. But it was a barren, dusty hillock.

When they surveyed the land, naysayers cried out, "Prabhu, we can't build a temple here. Look at the pollution; just see these thorny bushes."

Madhu Pandit kept quiet. Suddenly, he noticed a small patch with the sacred *tulsi* plant.

"This place is where the Lord will rest; it is destined for that."

For the next 8 years, Madhu Pandit and his fellow devotee Chanchalapathi Dasa worked tirelessly with a team of 50 dedicated volunteers to raise funds and oversee the construction of the temple complex.

It took 600 skilled craftsmen more than 10 million man-hours to construct this magnificent house of worship. 32,000 cubic metres of stone, 131,250 tons of cement and 1,900 tons of steel were used in the process.

The total cost was ₹32 crore — the entire amount collected by ISKCON volunteers going door to door. Mostly, small contributions of ₹5 and ₹10 from ordinary men and women.

But the man who climbed the temple steps on a Sunday morning in March 2000 was far from ordinary. He was one of the prime movers and shakers of an exciting new company called Infosys.

At the age of 41, Mohandas Pai was on top of the world.

He was the CFO of a large corporation, which had come far from its humble origins. The seven founders who quit their jobs at Patni Computer Systems had defied the odds to build India's most successful software services company.

'An exciting place to work at,' declared *The Economic Times*. 'Nobody wears a tie to office, the average age of employees is 24.'

Well, Mohan had not joined the company to enjoy pizza

parties. A hard-boiled finance professional, he was attracted to Infosys by the challenge of doing something big and bold.

"We want to list on the New York Stock Exchange," founder Narayana Murthy had bluntly stated in the interview.
"Can you do it?"

No Indian company had been listed on a foreign stock exchange.

"Yes, I certainly can," replied Mohan.

For the next 18 months, the young CFO worked day and night, constantly on the road. Meeting bankers and investors, convincing them to 'have faith' in a young and unknown company in the distant Indian city of Bangalore.

On 18th July 1999, Mohan and Narayana Murthy stood in Times Square to witness a special event. Four letters flashed across the screen of the NYSE ticker — I N F Y.

Choked with emotion Murthy turned to his CFO and said, "We did it!"

But somewhere within, Mohan felt restless. Would the next listing produce the same adrenaline rush? Would another award for 'best CFO' feel like an achievement? If this was really the peak of his career, why did he not feel truly happy?

As he pondered these questions, his fingers ran through some unopened mail. One of the envelopes bore the logo of ISKCON. It felt lumpy.

Mohan tore the envelope and found a sealed packet containing prasadam. 'Hare Krishna!' read the message. 'A small gift from the Lord on your birthday.'

Mohan squirmed guiltily. His birthday was last week, but he

had been too busy to even celebrate it with his family. His wife Kusum was still grumbling about it.

But the birthday greetings reminded Mohan of another commitment he had been unable to keep.

Two years ago, a monk by the name of Anand Teertha had visited his office to ask for 'Sudama Seva'. Mohan had willingly pledged to donate ₹5 per day to ISKCON towards temple construction.

While the devotee had forgotten his promise, the Lord had sent a gentle reminder.

"It's about time you visited me," he playfully whispered into Mohan's ear.

"I will, I will come to your abode very soon," promised Mohan.

It was a Sunday in the month of March, when Mohan finally kept that promise.

Wearing a khadi kurta and white pyjama, he joined the throng of pilgrims on the granite steps of the ISKCON temple.

The devotees were of every age and inclination. From *mamis* in bright silk saris to college students in t-shirt and jeans. Infants ran up and down, while their mothers scolded them in vain.

Mohan could have made one phone call to Anand Teertha and asked for 'VIP *darshan*'. Entry through a special side entrance, reserved for 'important folk' who did not care to stand in line.

But Mohan disliked the idea of special treatment.

Besides, he was enjoying the simple act of climbing up to the rhythmic chanting of the Hare Krishna *mantra*.

Hare Krishna Hare Krishna
Krishna Krishna Hare Hare
Hare Rama Hare Rama
Rama Rama Hare Hare

This chant is the cornerstone of ISKCON.

A movement founded by Srila Prabhupada, who travelled to America in 1966 with eight dollars in his pocket. He embarked on this perilous journey to fulfil the desire of his guru — to take the teachings of the *Bhagavad Gita* to the West.

In 11 short years, the founder–acharya had established 108 ISKCON temples across the world.

After Prabhupada's death in 1977, the ISKCON movement continued to grow and attract new followers. ISKCON temples were now being built in cities across India — each more magnificent than the other.

The Bangalore temple was one such shining example. In size and in vision, it surpassed any ordinary house of worship.

As he walked under the giant dome, Mohan's eyes were arrested by the frescos on the ceiling, depicting Lord Krishna in various forms.

In front of him were the stunning deities of Sri Sri Radha-Krishna, adorned in fine silks and jewels.

Mohan prostrated himself on the ground, in deference and in reverence. After a minute in communion with the Lord, he rose. A priest in orange robes applied tilak on Mohan's forehead with sandalwood paste.

He wound his way towards the exit, where an ISKCON

devotee with orange robes and shining eyes was cheerfully distributing khichdi prasadam.

The aroma of *khichdi* took Mohan back to his childhood. For a minute, he closed his eyes and thought of his *ajji* (grandmother) conducting her daily *puja*. How he used to wait for her to ring the bell and start distributing *pedhas*.

A tap on his shoulder brought Mohan out of his reverie.

It was Anand Teertha, smiling broadly. He exclaimed, "Mohan, what are you doing here! Why didn't you tell me you were coming?"

The man continued excitedly, "Now that you are here, I must take you to meet our President… Come with me!"

Swiftly navigating the temple complex, Anand Teertha led the visitor up a flight of marble stairs to the operational headquarters of ISKCON Bangalore.

There, in a large room with white walls and sparse furniture, under the photograph of A C Bhaktivedanta Swami Prabhupada, a tall, dark man in a crisp, cream-coloured *dhoti-kurta*, rose to greet his visitor. "*Namaskaram*, Mr Pai," said Madhu Pandit with a smile.

Anyone who saw Madhu Pandit rise to greet Mohan might have thought — "How very different are these two individuals!"

But beneath the outer garments and mannerisms were two men of the same mould.

Men of action. Men who could get things done.

CHAPTER 2

VICHAAR

Mohan eyed the imposing figure of Madhu Pandit curiously. The first words he uttered to Madhu were, "Please accept my apologies."

The ISKCON President was puzzled.

Mohan quickly added, "I pledged to give 'Sudama Seva' for two years but forgot all about it. I have come to fulfil my promise."

Madhu Pandit laughed heartily, "Yes, yes ... perhaps Lord Krishna should charge you with interest!"

But somewhere, he was touched. Mohandas Pai, CFO of a large and successful company like Infosys — such a humble and down-to-earth man!

"What will you have Mr Pai — ginger-lime juice or shall I call for Vedic tea? I am sorry, we do not serve normal tea or coffee here," said Madhu Pandit with a merry twinkle in his eyes.

Mohan had visited many temples and met many holy men. But there was something different about this swamiji.

"Your temple is very impressive," remarked Mohan. "It is very modern and yet so traditional. Who is the architect?"

Madhu Pandit smiled enigmatically.

"Prabhu has designed it himself," said a young monk standing next to him.

Now it was Mohan's turn to be surprised. How could this dhoti-clad swami with a long tilak on his forehead be the architect of such a massive and modern temple — impossible!

"I am a BTech from IIT Bombay, Mr Pai," said Madhu Pandit. "In fact most of our devotees at ISKCON Bangalore are either engineers or scientists, a highly educated lot. The Vice President, Chanchalapathi Dasa, is also from the Indian Institute of Science."

Mohan nodded along, but his veins pulsed with excitement. At last, at long last, he saw a ray of hope.

I must speak to Abhay Jain.

Mohan and Abhay were childhood friends. While Mohan came from a middle class family, Abhay was the son of a businessman. Mohan was brilliant while Abhay was an average student. Despite these differences, the two were inseparable in school.

Years later, Mohan and Abhay had reconnected and once again become close. Both were very successful — Mohan in the corporate world and Abhay in his family business. What they also shared was a desire to 'do something', to give back to society, to the country as a whole.

When Abhay and Mohan met at each other's homes, their discussions always came down to this. "What can we do Abhay, that will make a lasting impact?" Mohan would ask him. But neither had the answer.

The two friends had jointly contributed to a number of smaller causes. When the Principal of their alma mater (St Joseph's Indian High School) asked them to support the education of a few underprivileged students, Mohan and Abhay answered their teacher's call without a moment's hesitation. Similarly, they had also set up the Bangalore Sports Club in 1994, the largest club in Karnataka, which focused on nurturing athletes at the school level.

But for them, this was never enough. Over endless cups of tea, the two friends debated. And they concluded that education would have the largest impact on the people.

"We were lucky to study in a Jesuit institution, don't you think, Abhay?" mused Mohan. "We need to start schools in association with more such dedicated and selfless organisations."

With this objective in mind, Abhay approached several NGOs and religious societies. Urging them to take up this cause. But nobody was interested. The two friends had almost given up ... but now an idea was dancing in Mohan's head.

"What about ISKCON?" he said to Abhay. "They can infuse schoolchildren with an Indian spirit as well as a modern, scientific temper."

Abhay was well aware of ISKCON Bangalore and its dynamic President. The duo sought an appointment with Madhu Pandit the following Sunday. This time, Mohan came straight to the point.

"Swamiji, you have built a beautiful *mandir* — all this is very good — but what about the poor people, those who are not coming to this temple?"

Madhu Pandit was puzzled. The role of a temple, after all, is to attract devotees. To provide spiritual guidance to all who choose to receive it. Poverty alleviation or social work was outside the purview of temple work.

"What do you have in mind, Mr Pai?" asked Madhu Pandit, with curiosity.

"Why don't you start schools like the Jesuits do? Modern schools with Indian values. I will support you if you start this initiative."

Madhu Pandit and his deputy Chanchalapathi exchanged an alarmed glance.

"We cannot start schools," replied Chanchalapathi. "It is risky for us, it is beyond the scope of our work."

But Mohan was not one to give up so easily. He suggested a number of different ideas — sewing machines for women in slums, computer training for high school students.

Each time the monks politely said 'no'. For it did not strike a chord with their thinking.

Just as they were about to leave, Mohan suddenly thought of the *dona* of khichdi which he enjoyed each time he visited the temple.

"Why don't you start a mid-day meal program, Swamiji?" he burst out.

"Anyway you give all *bhakts* who visit the temple khichdi as prasadam. You can also distribute this khichdi in the local government schools."

Looking at everyone's confused expression, Mohan impatiently explained, "Did you know M G Ramachandran, who was CM of Tamil Nadu, had started a 'mid-day meal program' for the children of his state? It has achieved phenomenal results."
After the program was implemented, the kids were healthier, taller and had even gained weight. What's more, school dropout rates fell significantly.

"Feeding a child, Swamiji, is not charity. It is our collective duty," said Mohan.

Madhu Pandit, Chanchalapathi and Abhay listened intently as Mohan continued telling them about how MGR had initiated this progam because he knew how profoundly debilitating hunger was.

This time there was a glimmer of interest. The monks did not refuse outright. But they did not say 'yes' either.

"Think it over, Swamiji. I will come back to the temple again next Sunday. Give me your answer then."

After Mohan's visit, Madhu Pandit sat in his office in silent contemplation.

The following week he went to Kolkata for some work, but every time he spoke with Chanchalapathi Dasa, the same topic came up.

"Prabhu, we need to give Mohan an answer … once you return."

Here was an important leader from the corporate world asking him to start a social initiative that he was willing to support. The offer had to be considered seriously.

As they bounced the idea back and forth, the monks realised that feeding programs had always been part of ISKCON. In the early years, Srila Prabhupada was known to cook and distribute prasadam with his own hands. In the same spirit, ISKCON Bangalore conducted food distribution in slum areas on Janmashtami day.

"We even have a spare festival kitchen," observed Chanchalapathi.

By the time his visitors arrived the following week, Madhu Pandit had made his decision. The temple was ready to start feeding 1,500 schoolchildren.

"But I need three vehicles to transport the food."

Mohan, Abhay and their friend P N C Menon of Sobha Developers smiled at each other.

"Done," they said in unison.

There was no business plan, market study or excel sheet projection. Just a meeting of minds, flow of emotion.

Neither the 'angel investors' nor the 'founders' of this new enterprise knew what sleeping giant had been awakened.

CHAPTER 3

SANKALPA

That evening, Madhu Pandit summoned his trusted lieutenant Chanchalapathi to his office. They sat cross-legged on a straw mat, under the affectionate gaze of Srila Prabhupada.

The task before them was to put together a team. The first name that came to mind was Venu Vadana Gopala Dasa — a devotee who was managing the kitchen operations. Before joining ISKCON, he had run his own small business in Chennai.

"Add Vikram Krishna Dasa's name to the list as well, Prabhu," said Chanchalapathi.

Vikram Krishna was a very intelligent, very committed young man. He was a BSc gold medallist from MES College, and then — like so many others — he had stumbled upon Srila Prabhupada's treatise on the *Bhagavad Gita*. Soon after, Vikram turned his back on a lucrative corporate career to join ISKCON.

For men of such calibre, launching the mid-day meal program

was not a difficult task. But it was something new, hence certainly a challenge.

"This is a pilot project," said Madhu Pandit to his team. "We can cook the khichdi in our own kitchen, but which schools should we go to?"

The task of identifying these schools fell on Venu Vadana. On a hot afternoon in the month of May, he climbed into the temple auto-rickshaw and set off on a fact-finding expedition.

Venu Vadana's first stop was a small government school in Makali, a few kms from the ISKCON campus. As he neared his destination, the road grew bumpier and the rickshaw shook violently.

"Is this really Bangalore?" Venu Vadana thought to himself. The area looked very poor and underdeveloped.

Passing through shanties and piles of garbage, he could see in the distance a modest, whitewashed building. It was the largest building in the area, and Venu Vadana knew it had to be the school.

He wound his way to the headmaster's office, a small, dark room where a short, middle-aged man sat behind the desk. "Good afternoon, Sir," greeted Venu Vadana.

The headmaster looked up in surprise. Why had a monk come to his school, he wondered.

"Yes? What can I do for you?" he asked politely, gesturing to Venu Vadana to have a seat.

"Sir, I have come from the ISKCON temple to talk to you about a new program we are starting — a daily mid-day meal program for children."

The headmaster looked at him with interest.

"Daily? Are you sure, Swamiji? Will you really come daily to give food?"

"Yes, Sir. Every day we will give lunch. Do you think there is a need in your school for such a program?"

The headmaster stayed quiet for a while. Then, he gripped Venu Vadana's hand and said, "Swamiji, this is a very good thing you are doing. You don't know ... how much our children will benefit. Most of them don't get even one proper meal a day."

Like many slum colonies, Makali was populated by daily wage labourers. Even mothers worked on construction sites or as maidservants, and had no time to cook in the morning.

"You know what happens, Swamiji ... so many children faint in class. They cannot concentrate because they are always hungry."

Venu Vadana visited four other schools that afternoon. At each school the reaction was the same. First, disbelief, and then, the eager question: "When are you starting?"

It would be another fortnight before the first mid-day meal was actually served.

The 3rd of July 2000 was the auspicious day of the Rath Yatra festival. It was also the day chosen to launch the mid-day meal program.

A wave of steam mingled with the *masaaledar* smell of cooked khichdi greeted Achyutha Krishna Dasa as he entered the temple kitchen. Men in *lungis* and *banians* stood beside bubbling cauldrons, stirring the food.

Achyutha Krishna dipped a spoon into one cauldron and took out a small mouthful of khichdi to taste.

"Hmm," he smacked his lips. "It's tasty. Hopefully the children will like it too." As he swallowed the khichdi, he lovingly chanted a prayer in his mind.

Outside, men were hosing down the temple van, ready to start delivery.

Workers filled container after container with hot khichdi. Then, each heavy steel container was picked up by two men from either side, and loaded into the van.

Venu Vadana sat next to the driver to navigate the route. He was also eager to note how long it would take to reach each school.

At the back, Achyutha Krishna stood, nervously eyeing the hot, steel containers. With each bump and pothole, he tried valiantly to steady the containers. Still, hot, yellow khichdi spilled out, splashing and scalding the monk.

"Careful!" he yelled at the driver.

The van finally came to a stop at the first school. It was just after noon. The two monks unloaded three large containers of khichdi, and stacks of disposable thermocol plates.

As Achyutha Krishna started serving the hungry children, he remembered his mother, always coaxing him to 'eat well'. How lovingly she used to prepare his tiffin!

He placed extra helpings of khichdi on each plate.

The schoolroom had been noisy when they entered. Now the children were silent, relishing the warm and tasty lunch.

Achyutha Krishna had only recently joined the temple. He wasn't sure if this was really his calling. But then, he knew he could always return to his family after a few years. Srila Prabhupada always said that one could follow the principles of the *Gita* even as a householder.

The time at ISKCON would reveal to Achyutha Krishna what path his life would take.

As he pondered over this question, Achyutha Krishna felt a small fist tugging at his orange kurta. A sweet-faced, 10-year-old boy was looking at him with tears in his eyes.

"Will you come every day to give us food?" he asked softly.

Achyutha Krishna knelt down to face the boy.

"I have eaten only plain rice for three days," he whispered. "I like this food ... it is so tasty, and I like you also!"

Achyutha Krishna felt a lump growing in his throat. He placed his hand on the child's head and stroked his hair.

Many years later, he said, "This was the moment I realised I will never go back to the old life. These are my brothers and sisters; this is my family..."

Achyutha Krishna returned to the temple with empty vessels but a heart overflowing with love.

In those first few days and weeks, the food was cooked, it was transported, it was served. There was no great technology or scientific method.

It was a bunch of dedicated young men using their common sense. That's all you really need to do anything useful in this world.

CHAPTER 4

VIGHNA

On the eighth day after the feeding program had started, Venu Vadana came running up to Chanchalapathi and blurted, "Prabhu, what to do! Children are just not eating!"

The vessels with khichdi were returning half-filled. There was no demand for second helpings.

At an emergency meeting called in Madhu Pandit's office, it was decided to check the quality of food. Perhaps there was too much salt? Or *masala*?

"Maybe we should give some variety," said Chitranga Chaitanya Das. As the manager of the restaurant on the ISKCON Bangalore campus, he knew a thing or two about taste buds.

The following day it was decided to add a sweet dish. On the first day, it was *halwa*, on the second day *kesari bhath*. But the khichdi was still coming back — hardly eaten.

It was the headmaster of one of the schools who solved the

mystery. He said to Venu Vadana, "Swamiji, this is a school, not a marriage party. Give us simple food, what we eat at home!"

For khichdi is a novelty item in Karnataka. It is rice and *sambar* which forms the staple diet.

"This makes a lot of sense," said Madhu Pandit. The menu was quickly modified.

When stainless steel vessels bearing sambar-rice arrived at the school, there was a wave of excitement. Children ate with gusto, licking their fingers. They asked for more.

The real hit was a serving of fresh curds. A staple item that few households could afford.

Clearly, it was not rich and fancy food that the children craved. It was nutrition.

From then on, kitchen experiments were guided by that principle. The cooks came up with *bisi bele bhath* — an all-in-one local dish made with rice, *tur dal* and vegetables. Served piping hot, it was packed with taste, as well as protein and vitamins.

But every day brought a new challenge. On top of the list was the daily recurring cost, which nobody had anticipated.

Cutting down the quality of the food was not an option. But what about other areas? One wasteful expenditure was the use of disposable plates.

After consulting teachers, they arrived at a simple solution. Give each child a steel plate and ask him or her to bring it to school.

"They will take better care of it than we can," said the headmasters.

After eating, each child would wash their plate and carry it back home.

Distribution of food was another issue. The children sat in rows on the floor, in traditional Indian style. This required someone to go child-to-child, serving the food with a ladle.

Here, again, it was decided to make the operation self-sustaining. Older children would take turns to serve the food to younger ones.

"We have to modify the vessels — use smaller sizes — so that kids can lift them."

One of the trickiest parts was making sure the food reached each school on time. Venu Vadana would chalk out the route and then go with the driver to make sure he did not lose his way.

Every vehicle would have a driver and two helpers to load and unload the vessels. In addition, a security guard would be responsible for the quantity of food delivered.

"I will have a meeting with teachers and headmasters, how to sign a chart after counting the vessels. Because the same number they must return."

Mobile phones were relatively new — and expensive — but each vehicle was provided with one. To be used in case of emergencies.

Occasionally, a tyre would get punctured. The driver was instructed to take an auto and go to the nearest tempo stand. Transfer the food to another vehicle and ensure it reaches the schools.

"We will give ₹1,000 to every driver in the morning. As a contingency fund. And every evening we will take it back!"

At the weekly meeting with Madhu Pandit and Chanchalapathi, no issue was too small to discuss. And no problem was too big to solve.

After two months, the first of the three vehicles promised by Mohan and Abhay arrived. A gleaming Ashok Leyland truck bearing the ISKCON Bangalore logo on one side. A *gopuram* design on top of the vehicle added a distinctive touch.

Achyutha Krishna was in the kitchen supervising the transfer of rice into smaller vessels when someone ran up to him and said, "Leave this — come outside!"

Chanchalapathi was waiting there. He said, "I heard you can drive a car — is that correct?"

Achyutha Krishna nodded.

"Great! We don't have a driver for this vehicle today. Can you help out?"

Achyutha Krishna nodded dumbly. But he was shaking inside. Driving a Maruti 800 was very different from driving a truck!

Mumbling prayers under his breath, he turned the key in the ignition and, miraculously, managed to drive it.

Any entrepreneurial activity requires you to go beyond what you already do. What you already know. But change is not easy for everyone.

With more schools asking for the mid-day meal, the

program was growing rapidly. And so were problems in the temple kitchen.

Both mid-day meals as well as khichdi prasadam were being prepared on the same premises, which was now clearly inadequate. There was a constant 'traffic jam' on the work floor, with tempers boiling over like *rasam* from a cauldron.

"Who are these new fellows, eh?" grumbled the head cook of the temple. "How much rice they are cooking, more and more every day!"

The cooks hired by Akshaya Patra came at five in the morning and were still on the job when the temple hands arrived at 9 am. The older cooks felt like guests in their own kitchen.

"This is how it starts," muttered one veteran cook darkly. "First they come for a few days, then they take over everything. Soon we will have to beg them for utensils!"

Venu Vadana and Vikram Krishna were acutely aware of the simmering tension.

They tried to mitigate the situation by arranging for additional stoves and purchasing new vessels. In any case, the ever-increasing quantity of rice and sambar required bigger and bigger *bartans*.

One day, Venu Vadana exclaimed in exasperation, "Prabhu, where will we find a *dekchi* large enough to cook for all our children at once!"

Indeed, the traditional cooking method was proving to be highly inefficient. Surely there must be a better way to get the job done?

At the daily evening meeting with Madhu Pandit, Vikram Krishna proposed, "Prabhu, let us design a new and modern kitchen!"

The idea was quickly accepted, but now the question was, how does one go about building such a kitchen? What is the technology that can be used?

"We must go and see how other large kitchens operate," said Madhu Pandit. "Let us make a trip to Dharmasthala."

For excellence is a quest. You learn from everywhere and everyone, but deep in your heart, you aspire to be even better.

CHAPTER 5

PRERANA

On a humid August evening, four monks boarded the Karwar Express at Bangalore.

"These days I see rice and sambar even in my dreams," joked Vikram Krishna as he settled into the top berth. Chanchalapathi chuckled from below.

Madhu Pandit and Venu Vadana were already asleep — it had been another long and tiring day.

While the rest of the passengers lay asleep, the monks rose at 4 am, as was their habit. By the time Mangalore junction arrived, their daily *sadhana* was complete.

The four of them disembarked and boarded a bus to Dharmasthala, 74 kms away.

Dharmasthala (which literally means 'place of dharma') is a famous temple town on the banks of the Nethravathi river in Dakshina Kannada district of Karnataka. Thousands of devotees visit this temple for darshan of Lord Shiva and Lord Manjunatha, as well as the Dharma Daivas (guardian spirits of Dharma), namely Kalarahu, Kalarkayi, Kumaraswamy and Kanyakumari.

The average flow of pilgrims is about 10,000 people a day. As per tradition, each and every visitor is offered *anna daan* (free food). The massive task of feeding these pilgrims is managed with the help of a modern, mechanised kitchen.

A tour of this kitchen was the main agenda for this trip.

After a quick bath at the guesthouse, the monks headed straight to the Shri Manjunatha temple for darshan.

"I am feeling hungry now!" mumbled Venu Vadana. Indeed, in all the excitement, they had only consumed a couple of bananas for breakfast.

It was noon and the Annapoorna dining hall was already packed with pilgrims eagerly awaiting their meal. For there is a popular saying in Kannada, "If you do not take prasad after your darshan, your *yatra* (pilgrimage) is not complete."

Indeed, the more practical aspect is that when you visit Dharmasthala, you should focus on prayers and meditation, not on mundane questions like 'where to stay' and 'where to eat'. The temple will provide for that.

The four hungry pilgrims from Bangalore knew exactly where to go.

As they entered the dining hall, Chanchalapathi was awestruck. What size! What scale! Row upon row of men, women and children were seated on the floor, eating with relish from banana leaf plates. Nimble-footed boys with lungis tucked in at their waist scurried up and down the aisles with buckets of piping hot food.

Sambar? Rice?

The servers bent down to pour ladlefuls of steaming sambar onto glittering white mounds of rice. Until the patron indicated 'enough' by covering the plate with a hand.

Venu Vadana, Vikram Krishna, Madhu Pandit and Chanchalapathi thoroughly enjoyed the meal. They washed down the rice and sambar with creamy, freshly-made buttermilk.

"The kootu is so tasty and crunchy," remarked Venu Vadana, making a mental note to introduce this cucumber salad into the Akshaya Patra menu.

What fascinated Vikram Krishna was the speed of the entire operation.

"If I am correct, it takes just 12 to 13 minutes to seat, serve, eat, clean and start the next meal service."

Later, when they met Dr Harshendra Kumar, Chief Operating Officer of the kitchen and dining hall, he confirmed the rough calculation was correct.

"Our dining hall is 19,800 square feet with nine seating areas; we call them bays. Each bay can feed 400 people at a time. By the time the seventh row has been seated and served, it's time to clean the first row. This ensures that there is never a long queue to enter the dining hall."

"How many pilgrims visit Dharamasthala every day?" asked Venu Vadana.

"Daily, at least 10,000, but during the Lakshadeep festival in

October, it goes up to 100,000 people."

"Hare Krishna!" mumbled Chanchalapathi. Nothing could be more exciting than a peep into the kitchen which conducted this gigantic exercise, day after day, month after month.

Reading the visitors' minds, Dr Kumar offered them a tour of his mega kitchen. As they entered, the aroma of freshly-ground spices wafted to their noses. Two dozen workers were busy chopping cabbages and tomatoes, while a handful were bent over grinding machines, wrestling with the all-important coconut.

"Here ... you see ... every day we chop 4,000 kgs of vegetables…"

"45 kgs of spices make 3,000 litres of sambar…"

"Rice? Oh, at least 6,000 to 8,000 kgs a day. Or even more than that."

But how does one cook such enormous quantities? The mystery was revealed when Dr Kumar pointed to a giant stainless steel steam boiler.

Venu Vadana, Vikram Krishna and Chanchalapathi were smiling from ear to ear. This was the 'Holy Grail' they had been searching for.

The next morning, they met Dr Veerendra Heggade, Dharmadhikari, whose family has been looking after the temple for 21 generations.

"It is both a privilege and a responsibility," he said solemnly.

Dr Heggade arranged a tour of the temple storehouse, an industrial-size building where all the fresh produce, grain and spices were stored.

"We still follow the age-old traditions here," said the *musaddi* (store manager), pointing out the *tuladhari* (man with weighing scale) and *shanbaug* (book-keeper using pen and paper).

The visitors were shown the process of *tulabharam*, where devotees offer donations of rice, jaggery and coconut equal to their body weight.

They saw the temple plantations, on which grew everything from rice to coconut and betel nut.

There was even a dairy farm with 125 cows, which supplied most of the temple's daily milk requirement.

"This is complete backward integration," thought Vikram Krishna.

But the most impressive of all was the waste management system. Every day the cooking of rice generated 3,000 to 5,000 litres of starchy water. This was sent into the feeding tubs of the cattle to supplement their diet.

Kitchen waste in the form of vegetable peels and leftovers was sent to a compost pit. Generating over 1 lakh kgs of organic fertiliser annually. This, in turn, was used in the plantations to produce rice and jaggery, betel nut and coconut.

"We can't have our own cows and farms but we can do something with our kitchen waste," said Venu Vadana.

Mission accomplished, the four weary visitors paid a

courtesy visit to their hosts.

"Thank you," said Madhu Pandit. "After seeing your kitchen, your steam boilers, we feel confident. Akshaya Patra can definitely feed 10,000 children!"

The hosts exchanged a wry look. One of them said, "Think carefully before you start any feeding program…. Once you start, you can never stop!"

The monks looked at each other knowingly. Three months ago, they had started of feeding 1,500 children. Now it was close to 10,000! Where would the money come from?

Back in Bangalore, Madhu Pandit began pacing up and down, mulling over this very question. The CEO of a spiritual enterprise was in dire need of growth capital.

CHAPTER 6

SWAPNA

"ISKCON to start feeding 30,000 children."

Madhu Pandit stared at the newspaper headline in shock. What had he been thinking!

The reporter had asked, "What are your future plans?"

And perhaps to impress him, Madhu Pandit declared, "We want to feed 30,000 children."

Now seeing the figure in cold hard print, it hit him. Sure, there was a desire to do more, but no firm plan or date! Already, they were under pressure....

A pile of applications was lying on Madhu Pandit's desk. In less than two months, dozens of headmasters were requesting, "Come to our school."

"More than 1 lakh children need our mid-day meal!" muttered Madhu Pandit under his breath.

Hare Krishna, so many hungry stomachs ... is it the job of

my temple to feed them all?

That night, the President of ISKCON Bangalore could not sleep. He turned to Prabhupada for solace. The book he chose contained a story. And it could not be a coincidence.

The story read as follows:

Once Srila Prabhupada was in Mayapur, the birthplace of Chaitanya Mahaprabhu. On the day of Prana Prathishtha, there was a feast at the ISKCON temple. Soon after, there was a commotion outside the gate. Prabhupada went to find out what was happening.

He saw a garbage bin overflowing with banana leaf plates. Some of them contained leftover bits of food. The village children were fighting with dogs for this food.

Srila Prabhupada was moved to tears. He arranged for the distribution of prasadam.

He later declared, "No one should go hungry within a ten-mile radius of any ISKCON temple."

To Madhu Pandit, it was an SMS from the universe.

Go ahead without fear. It is the Lord's will.

The next morning, Madhu Pandit emerged with his spiritual battery 100% charged. Now, he turned to the matters of the mundane world. Costing, planning, implementation — the path of *karma*.

Designing a bigger, better kitchen was the first priority. He summoned Vikram Krishna. The two engineering brains began whirring.

"Prabhu, I have contacted the same company which supplies steam boilers to Dharmasthala," said Vikram Krishna. "The maximum capacity is 800 litres."

That would not suffice. For the entire day's cooking had to be done in a matter of hours.

"We need bigger boilers! Tell them we need a capacity of 1,200 litres."

The monks looked into each and every detail so as to improve the workflow. And ensure hygiene. Stainless steel vessels, granite floors. And a high-pressure washing system to sanitise the kitchen after the day's cooking.

Unlike Dharmasthala, there was a limitation of space on the ISKCON campus. And there was the additional task of packing.

"It is difficult to move hot food into smaller containers," said the helpers.

"Prabhu, the rice too is a problem … it is sticking together," was a daily complaint.

When there is no model to 'copy', you must ponder. And then, improvise.

Ultimately, they devised a 'vibrator machine' so that the cooked grain would get pushed downward.

At the final stages, vessels with piping hot foods would be moved for delivery on a conveyor belt.

A back-of-the-envelope calculation put the cost of this 'dream kitchen' at a whopping ₹1 crore. And feeding 30,000 children meant a recurring cost of ₹40 lakh per month.

"What will Mohan say when I tell him!"

"Swamiji, India is a country of scale," said Mohan.

The CFO of Infosys was delighted. Here, at last, was someone he didn't have to push. To think bold, to think big.

"Don't worry, we will help you with fundraising," assured Mohan.

Indeed, Abhay and Mohan were spending every waking moment outside of work on the mid-day meal program. Creating awareness among their wide network of contacts.

For Mohan, this included business associates. Anyone who visited him at Infosys was promptly sent across to ISKCON.

"You will see something amazing!" he promised.

The task of making the 'sales pitch' was assigned to Chanchalapathi. He took the job seriously, consulting thick reports by the United Nations on 'malnutrition' and 'hunger'. A PowerPoint presentation was put together. With facts, with figures, and above all, an emotional appeal.

One of the stories Chanchalapathi sometimes told was that of the 'sack of rice'.

Srila Prabhupada used to say: If you leave a sack of rice on the ground, birds will come, take a few grains and fly away. But if a human being comes, he will pick up the entire bag and run away.

Because of greed, people hoard much more than what they need. And, as a result, there is inequity. There is starvation. The farmer toils to produce food but his own children go hungry.

"We are all interconnected and we must all share — this will be our message!"

Saturday and Sunday saw the maximum visitors. Chanchalapathi would make the same presentation five times in a single day.

Slowly but surely, they were building a brand.

These interactions were not just one-way. For Chanchalapathi was always open to learning from other people. One day, he received a foreign visitor, a social scientist.

The man asked, "What is the impact of your program?" Impact? Nobody at ISKCON Bangalore had thought in such terms. Chanchalapathi went back that evening and read up all he could.

"I need to include this idea of 'impact' in my presentations from now on."

One day, there would be full-fledged impact studies. For a seed had been planted, in a mind fertile....

While Mohan's circle consisted of professionals and businessmen, Abhay was acquainted with bureaucrats and politicians. Who were important in their own way.

One morning, Abhay arrived at the temple and said, "Please pack a tiffin carrier with prasadam and come with me."

He took them to the guesthouse of the National Aeronautics Laboratory (NAL) in Bellandur. There, they met Dr Murli Manohar Joshi, then Union Minister for Human Resource Development.

With a trademark red tilak on his forehead, Dr Joshi received the visitors with great respect. Madhu Pandit and Chanchalapathi were tongue-tied. It was the first time they were meeting a Union minister. They let Mohan and Abhay do the talking.

Mohan said, "We started with just 1,500 children but now

1 lakh children want this mid-day meal. There is so much hunger…. The task is endless!"

"Ah," said Dr Joshi. "So your program is like the 'Akshaya Patra' from the *Mahabharata*."

There was a moment of silence in the room. In vain, they had been searching for a name for this mid-day meal program. Akshaya Patra was perfect!

For every Indian child knows the story of the rice bowl blessed by Krishna. Which produces endless rice.

In economics, there is demand, there is supply, and there are 'market forces'.

But the Chief Economist is invisible and omnipresent. The Force behind all forces.

CHAPTER 7

PRAKRIYA

On 11 November 2000, the temple bore a festive air.
The ISKCON mid-day meal program was 'formally'
inaugurated by Dr Murli Manohar Joshi.

As he cut the ceremonial ribbon, Madhu Pandit and
Chanchalapathi beamed from ear to ear.

"Prabhu, everything went off very well," said
Chanchalapathi.

Rarely had so many VIPs of this stature visited the temple.
It was something they would have to get used to....

One morning, Madhu Pandit remarked in exasperation, "All
these politicians never used to give us an audience ... now they
all want an appointment with me!"

Local MLAs could see the impact of the mid-day meal
wherever it was being served.

"You must start the mid-day meal in my constituency!" they

requested. And the demands kept coming.

By June 2001, Akshaya Patra was feeding 13,000 children in and around the city. The 51st school to be covered was the R Gopalaswamy Iyer Government High School in Srirampura. A function was organised to celebrate this milestone.

The Minister for Education exhorted, "Our PM should start this scheme throughout the country!"

The audience clapped politely.

The Commissioner of Education, T M Vijay Bhaskar, also spoke on the occasion. The IAS officer said there was a scheme to give 3 kgs of rice or wheat to children in government schools (up to Class 5).

"From now on, we will give the rice to ISKCON so they can use it for the Akshaya Patra program."

The audience cheered this announcement lustily. Madhu Pandit and Chanchalapathi were also elated. At their weekly meetings, the main topic of discussion was the recurring cost of the meal program.

"Nowadays I get excited if the price of tomatoes falls," joked Chanchalapathi. "Just like a housewife!"

For each day, the kitchen consumed 556 kgs of vegetables, 1,500 kgs of rice and 1,223 litres of curd. The cost per meal was around ₹6 — a total of ₹78,000 per day.

Luckily, there was a team of fundraisers to fall back upon. A grand temple had been built through door-to-door collections. Now, that very method was used to raise funds for Akshaya Patra.

'Donate ₹1,200. Feed a child for one whole year,' read the

pamphlets.

Despite these efforts, there was always a shortfall. At such times, Madhu Pandit did not hesitate to dip into the temple *hundi*.

"People are donating to the temple out of piety. And nothing can be more pious than the temple feeding a hungry child," thought Madhu Pandit.

A few kms away, in the Infosys office, Mohan was echoing the same thought.

"Barbara, please despatch this cheque!" he said.

Mohan's trusted secretary nodded a 'yes'. Her boss could be tough, he could be gruff, but she would not choose to work for anyone else.

She put the cheque into the 'out' tray. It was a donation to Akshaya Patra. Barbara shook her head in disbelief. How could anyone donate their entire salary, every month, month after month?

"I wonder what his wife has to say," thought Barbara. But wisely, she never asked the boss.

As the CFO of Infosys, Mohan spent a great deal of time with auditors. One of the frequent visitors to his office was KPMG partner Prabhakar Kalavacherla. 'PK' to friends.

"PK, you spend so much time in my office I think you should just put your name on the door," said Mohan in a lighter vein one afternoon.

PK had recently shifted to Bangalore from the US and was still finding his feet. After completing his chartered accountancy in Hyderabad, PK did his CPA from California State University. Now, he was back in India after a long stint abroad.

"You know, Mohan," said PK, "I miss many things about America. But one thing I don't miss is the food!"

The two men were having a quick working lunch that day, which included PK's favourite, *dahi sadam* (curd rice).

"PK, you must come with me to Akshaya Patra. The food is better than the Infosys cafeteria!"

And soon, Mohan found a professional reason for PK to make that trip. He requested PK to audit Akshaya Patra's operations.

It was an interesting idea, something PK had never done. KPMG agreed to take up the project on a pro-bono basis.

"I must say, it's a pleasant surprise!" he said, after the audit was completed.

The KPMG team applied the standards used for any company in the food industry. And Akshaya Patra had passed with flying colours.

All expenses of Akshaya Patra were booked in the ISKCON temple account. This was working quite well, but Madhu Pandit's instinct was to go a step further.

"Everyone is not comfortable donating to temples," he said to Mohan at their next meeting. "If we want large corporates to support this program, it must be completely secular."

Mohan agreed. It would indeed be easier to manage Akshaya Patra as a separate entity.

"Mohan, let us set up a new trust. It will take some time, but let me start the paperwork."

The Akshaya Patra trust was registered in October 2001. A social experiment was now a legal entity with a stated mission and purpose. And a common platform for two very diverse sets of people.

The board of trustees included Madhu Pandit Dasa, Chanchalapathi Dasa and Chitranga Chaitanya Dasa from ISKCON Bangalore. They were spiritualists, running the program in the spirit of service.

The other set of members were capitalists who wanted to solve a big problem. This included Mohandas Pai, Abhay Jain and other eminent professionals.

The first to join was Raj Kondur, a Harvard Business School alumnus. He was originally from an agricultural family in Chintamani, a small town in rural Karnataka.

At 28, Raj Kondur had launched the high-profile VC firm Chrysalis Capital, only to quit two years later. During a sabbatical he spent some time at Infosys, and impressed the CFO.

"It will be good to have someone with an entrepreneur's mindset on our board," thought Mohan.

He then approached a trusted colleague, Ramadas Kamath, who shared some of Mohan's ideas. They had worked together earlier, to set up the Bangalore Sports Club.

"Akshaya Patra needs you," said Mohan to his good friend

and fellow Chartered Accountant.

Mohan also persuaded his Infy colleague Venkatraman Balakrishnan, or Bala, to become a trustee. A financial whiz, Bala had worked closely with Mohan at the time of the Infosys IPO.

Every individual on the board brought something unique to the table. What they did not bring was an ego. But this did not mean there were no disagreements.

Mostly, over how fast Akshaya Patra should grow.

"Once we cross 30,000, our next goal should be 100,000 children!" declared Mohan.

Abhay shook his head in disbelief. And auditor PK could not help an outburst.

"Mohan, everyone wants to grow but where is the corpus! You are taking a very big risk…"

Mohan knew that his friend PK was absolutely right. No organisation in its right mind spends all the money it earns — and commits to spend more — with no cash reserves in hand.

But Mohan was now beyond logic and rationality. He had entered the realm of faith.

Far from the cool climes of Bangalore, in the city of Jaipur, a chain of events was about to be set in motion. Which would prove him right.

CHAPTER 8

NYAYA

76, Shanti Niketan is Kavita Srivastava's home in Jaipur city. As the General Secretary of the People's Union for Civil Liberties (PUCL), Kavita's home is always an 'open house'.

Numerous friends, well-wishers, thinkers and activists would gather for meals and *gupshup*. On that fateful morning in the summer of 2001, Supreme Court lawyer Colin Gonsalves had dropped by for breakfast. So had economist-activist Jean Dreze.

Over *pyaaz-kachori* and *adrak chai*, the conversation suddenly veered towards hunger.

"You people have no idea what is happening in this country!" said Jean Dreze darkly.

On the spur of the moment, a bunch of those present got into a jeep and drove out of Jaipur city. And sure enough, you could see malnutrition, raw and naked. It was everywhere.

Jean Dreze explained the situation, "This is what we call

hunger amidst plenty!"

For there were 60 million tonnes of grain lying in godowns in India, enough to make a straight line to the moon and back. Yet, children were dying of hunger.

How could any government allow this to happen — to its own citizens?

Colin Gonsalves was deeply moved. The IIT Bombay graduate had shifted from civil engineering to law to make a difference to society. In 1989, Colin set up the Human Rights Law Network. To champion the cause of the underdog — to represent the weak and the exploited.

"Let us file a Public Interest Litigation in the Supreme Court," he suggested.

The petition began by referring to the 'innumerable cases of starvation deaths reported across the country largely due to non-availability of food to people over a long period of time'.

The petitioner sought directions to the state of Rajasthan and the Union of India to enforce the 'Famine Codes' and immediately release food grains lying in public godowns.

Colin admitted to his colleagues that he was not very hopeful. A similar petition filed in 1996 by social activist Kishen Pattanayak against the state of Orissa had been dismissed.

But there was nothing to lose — it was certainly worth trying!

Mondays and Fridays are the days when the Supreme Court hears 'fresh matters'. An average of 70 cases come up for hearing and each lawyer gets around one minute to present his/her case.

But when the Right to Food case came up for hearing, Colin did not even have to argue. Justice Kirpal opened the papers and remarked, "This cannot be…. We cannot allow this!"

A show cause notice was issued to the respondents and Attorney General Soli Sorabjee was asked to appear on behalf of the Union of India. There was much reason to cheer!

The Human Rights Law Network team worked night and day. With support from PUCL and Jean Dreze. In a record time of only three months, a landmark judgment was passed.

On 28 November 2001, the Supreme Court of India ruled that the Union of India must take immediate measures to make food grains available through the Public Distribution System, Antyodaya Anna Yojana and Integrated Child Development Scheme. It must also implement the Mid-Day Meal Scheme.

Every child in every government and government-assisted primary school must get a cooked mid-day meal with minimum 300 calories and 8-12 grams of protein for a minimum of 200 days.

The order took the government by surprise. For hundreds of its schemes existed only on paper.

"Had we delayed even by a year, the mid-day meal would have been officially closed," said Colin, feeling both relieved and overjoyed.

But this time, not only did the Supreme Court pass an order, it put pressure for implementation. Dr N C Saxena and Mr S R Sankaran were appointed as Commissioners to collect information from across the country. To verify that the schemes were actually working!

And on several occasions, the chief secretaries of different states were summoned and reprimanded.

This was bad news for lazy politicians and corrupt

headmasters. But good news for Akshaya Patra. Opening the doors for the Public–Private Partnership (PPP) model.

Now, in addition to food grains, the government was going to allot a sum of approximately ₹2 per child as 'cooking cost'.

"Instead of ₹6 per meal, our cost will now be ₹4 per meal!" cried Chanchalapathi, overcome with happiness.

In the PPP model, Akshaya Patra was able to scale up to 43,000 children by April 2003. This did not go unnoticed. One morning, Abhay received a call from Sudheendra Kulkarni, a close aide of then Prime Minister Atal Bihari Vajpayee.

"I am writing Atalji's Independence Day speech. Can you come to Delhi?"

At that time, Abhay's father was very ill and had been admitted to hospital. This put him in a quandary.

"What if I go to Delhi and my father passes away in Bangalore…." thought Abhay.

On the other hand, you do not say 'no' to a meeting in the Prime Minister's Office.

"Go ahead … nothing will happen to him while you're gone," assured the doctors. And so, keeping faith, Abhay and Mohan flew to Delhi.

In the meeting, Sudheendra Kulkarni said, "The Prime Minister is rolling out the Mid-Day Meal Scheme nationally. On his behalf, I am asking you, can we name it 'Akshaya Patra'?"

Mohan and Abhay happily consented. And fortunately, when Abhay returned to Bangalore in the evening, he found his father's condition unchanged.

On 15 August 2003, Atal Bihari Vajpayee announced:

The Mid-Day Meal Scheme for children up to Class 5 is going on in some states. Now, we have decided to run it throughout the country. Later, this will be extended to students up to Class 10. This National Program will be known as 'Akshaya Patra'. I appeal to voluntary organisations, religious establishments and women's self-help groups to come forward to implement this program in an effective way.

For three years, the organisation had toiled and proved its worth. Now, with the PM's blessing, the Akshaya Patra model would be adopted across the country.

"Finally, we will be able to serve the children in all parts of India," thought Madhu Pandit.

But a roll of the electoral dice can change destiny. That dice rolled against the NDA government in the summer of 2004.

Opportunity is like a cloud: sometimes it appears on the horizon and simply passes by; then, when you least expect it, there is a downpour.

This is what happened with Akshaya Patra.

0119004 3320

दिनांक/DATE 23 May, 03

PAY The Akshaya Patra Foundation, New Delhi

या धारक को OR BEARER

रुपये RUPEES Twelve thousand only

अदा करें

₹.Rs. 12,000/-

सं.सं.
A/c. No.

ब.प.,
L.F.

ह.ह.
INTLS.

भारतीय स्टेट बैंक
STATE BANK OF INDIA

सेंट्रल सेक्रटेरियट, नई दिल्ली - 110 001
CENTRAL SECRETARIATE, NEW DELHI -110001

MSBL/267

A.P.J. Abdul Kalam

"831906" 1000 20 14:   10

CHAPTER 9

VISTAAR

On 7 June 2003, there was an air of excitement at the ISKCON complex. The President of India, Dr A P J Abdul Kalam was scheduled to visit.

This time it was the monks who were taken by surprise, for Dr Kalam — a practicing Muslim — toured the temple. He not only took darshan of the deities, but waited for the *pujari* to give him blessings from the altar.

Dr Kalam remarked: "By seeing Them (the deities), one's sins and sorrows are washed away."

The President unveiled a plaque announcing the upscaling of the Akshaya Patra program from 43,000 children to 100,000 children by the end of the year.

The 'People's President' struck up an instant rapport with the kids. He sat with them and had lunch on a banana leaf, eating rice and sambar with his fingers.

Prasad, a 13-year-old from Uttarahalli Government School, was seated next to Dr Kalam.

"Sir, I want to become an engineer like you!" said the welder's son.

"Be a good boy," replied the former scientist. "Work hard and make your dream come true."

During the function, Dr Kalam praised the Akshaya Patra program. But he suggested adding one more dimension.

"This is the pot of *anna* (food)," he said, pointing to the Akshaya Patra logo. "We need one more pot — the pot of *vidya* (education)"

That very morning, the results of the 10th Standard board exams had been declared. Only 9% of the students in Bangalore Mahanagara Palike schools were declared 'pass'.

"How can we allow this to happen in the IT city of India!" said Dr Kalam.

It was a simple remark, but it struck a chord.

Four months later, with the help of well-wishers, the Vidya Akshaya Patra program was launched.

Funding came from Kris Gopalakrishnan of Infosys, while Shukla Bose — founder of Parikrama School — designed the free tutorial program.

"Let us focus on the schools that have the lowest pass percentage," she suggested.

A dozen municipal schools with 0–40% pass percentage were selected for the pilot program; 32 teachers and four coordinators worked with 1,024 students after school and on Sundays.

The pot of vidya was now a reality. But the pot of anna was not forgotten.

"Children will be hungry after school," said Chanchalapathi. "We will provide snacks."

For hungry minds work best on full stomachs.

Vyompada Dasa sat in a small shed in the holy city of Vrindavan and surveyed the day's cooking. It was time to load the cycle rickshaw and send off the mid-day meal to the government school of Gopalgarh.

Like many other ISKCON monks, Vyompada was highly educated. He was once an engineer with Motorola. Influenced by the books of Srila Prabhupada, he had dedicated himself to the service of Krishna.

Initially, Vyompada worked in ISKCON's publication department. Later, he assisted Venu Vadana at the Akshaya Patra kitchen in Bangalore.

"If we are starting a kitchen outside Bangalore, it has to be in Vrindavan," Madhu Pandit had declared emphatically. And the task of setting it up had fallen on Vyompada's young shoulders.

It was one thing to run a kitchen in Bangalore — a predictable and well-oiled machine. But here in Vrindavan, there was nobody to turn to. Even the mobile phone signal was a challenge.

And north India was very different from south India.
Three days after starting the mid-day meal program in
Vrindavan, a student got up and complained, "*Dal khatti hai*!"
(The dal is sour).

People in north India do not consume sambar. And their
staple diet is roti, not rice. The next day he called the cook and
instructed him in broken Hindi, "*Aaj se chapati.*"

At first, they were feeding just 100 children. Two women
could roll out the required chapatis with ease. But as the
numbers grew, it became a challenge.

"We can't make more and more chapatis by hand,"
Vyompada said to his seniors in Bangalore. "Isn't there a better
way to do it?"

The question acquired more urgency when Vasundhara
Raje, Chief Minister of Rajasthan, invited Akshaya Patra to
Jaipur for a meeting.

At that time, the government mid-day meal in Rajasthan
was a watery wheat gruel called *ghughri*, which the children
refused to eat.

This was obviously not acceptable!

In November 2003, Mohan, Abhay, PK and Chanchalapathi
arrived at the CM's residence. Vasundhara Raje requested the
visitors to wait while she completed her daily ritual of tulsi puja.

"Tell me, Swamiji — what is this Akshaya Patra? I have
heard so much about it from Abhay!"

When Chanchalapathi completed his presentation,
Vasundhara Raje clapped her hands and exclaimed, "This is the
first time I have seen a monk using computers.... You are not a

swami, you are technoswami!

"Give them all possible assistance. I want Akshaya Patra to start the mid-day meal program in Rajasthan!" declared Vasundhara Raje.

An IAS officer present at this meeting approached Ratnangada Govinda Dasa, the young monk deputed to set up the pilot kitchen.

"Swamiji, I come from a very poor family," he said. "I know the pain of sitting in school on an empty stomach. *Jo madad aapko chahiye main karne ko taiyyar hoon.*"

True to his word, the IAS officer personally took him to inspect four to five different locations. They were all unused or underused government buildings. But none of them fit the requirement.

Finally, they came to the Engineers Staff Training Institute in Jhalana Dungri. Situated in the middle of a small forest on the outskirts of the city, the building had two large halls, a kitchen and a store.

Ratnangada Govinda broke into a smile, "This is perfect."

State after state opened their doors for Akshaya Patra's nationwide expansion. In 10 short years, the program would be feeding a million children every day.

And as every entrepreneur knows, scaling up is 10 times harder than starting…

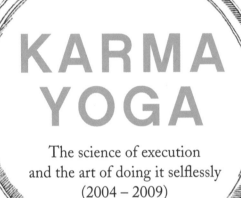

KARMA YOGA

The science of execution
and the art of doing it selflessly
(2004 – 2009)

CHAPTER 10

YANTRA

Ratnangada Govinda was sweating profusely. It was just six in the morning but already the temperature outside had crossed 40°C.

"Swamiji, Heerabai and Badambai are not coming today!" informed the kitchen supervisor. "We will be 500 chapatis short … *kya karein?*"

This was becoming a daily headache. The delivery of food would get delayed. On such days Ratnangada Govinda would often sit in the kitchen and help roll out chapatis himself.

The women giggled, "Rotiyon gol gol *wanavni … O aadmiyan ro kom koni.*" (You need to make round chapatis … this is not a man's job).

As a monk, Ratnangada Govinda had no such reservations. But he was no kitchen expert for sure. When he first arrived in Jaipur he did not even know how to switch on a gas stove.

The family he stayed with was very kind. During the day Ratnangada Govinda was busy meeting government officials, overseeing the kitchen construction. In the evening, he became a student.

"Swamiji, *aapko bhi to khana banana aana chahiye!*" said the lady of the house. And proceeded to teach him the basics of north Indian cooking.

In the two months it took to kick off the kitchen, Ratnangada Govinda had learnt the ka-kha-ga of cooking. What's more, a nephew who often visited that house became his friend.

"Swamiji, *aap jo kaam kar rahe ho mujhe pasand hai.* Will you take me as your assistant?"

And thus Ratnangada Govinda recruited the first employee of Akshaya Patra Jaipur. He knew the local language and culture and this was a big help in many ways. One daily chore was the purchase of vegetables. The idea was to buy what was in season, fresh and cheap.

"*Sabzi khareedne ka kaam mera,*" he said. "I can bargain and get a better price in the mandi."

One problem the Jaipur kitchen encountered early on was getting good workers. Jhalana Doongri was outside the city — both water and electricity was scarce in the area. And those who lived far from the kitchen were perennially late.

Madhu Pandit thought back to his own student days. In hostel, your neighbour ensures you get to class on time.

"Set up living quarters on the first floor, right above the kitchen," he instructed.

It was an out-of-the-box solution, and it worked. But now that workers were living on the campus, what would they do after the shift? Sports was one activity that would keep them busy.

Ratnangada Govinda purchased some cricket bats, footballs and volleyballs. It was a big morale booster.

"We can also start some vocational programs and take care of their health."

But now there was a problem for which there was no easy solution — the sweltering Jaipur heat. Made five degrees worse by the numerous chapati tawas. Workers were bunking work and falling sick.

"Now I know what it feels like inside a pressure cooker!" Ratnangada Govinda exclaimed to his seniors in Bangalore. "Can we install some coolers?"

Even if that could be done — what about the workers' health? Their hands had become coarse and black. Some were even having breathing problems.

Madhu Pandit said, "We need to put our heads together and find a solution. Isn't there an automatic roti-making machine at the Golden Temple?"

Like knights in quest of the Holy Grail, the monks set off for the holy city of Amritsar.

Ik onkar satnaam karta purakh nirbh-a-o...

The sweet melody of the mool mantra welcomed Vyompada and Chitranga Chaitanya as they entered Harmandir Sahib. It was early evening and the temple was glowing in the fading sunlight.

The monks removed their shoes and washed their feet. Covering their heads with scarves, they entered the Golden Temple, the holiest of holy Sikh shrines.

"It is so peaceful here..." thought Chitranga Chaitanya as he entered the Darbar. The Adi Granth was placed on a raised platform, covered with fine silk cloth.

The monks remained silent as they completed a *parikrama* of the Amrit Sarovar. The reflection of the Golden Temple in its still waters was as beautiful as the temple itself.

It was only after eating the *kadha prashad* that Vyompada came back to earth, "Oho, this is the tastiest halwa I have ever eaten! What could be the recipe?"

"We will ask the cook," winked Chitranga Chaitanya. For now came the 'work' part of this trip — a tour of the Golden Temple kitchen.

Thanks to B Swarup, a CBDT member and an advisor to Akshaya Patra, they had got the necessary permission.

The Golden Temple is famous for its *langar*, or community kitchen, established from the time of Guru Nanak. While there are 18 chefs, most of the kitchen work and the serving of food is done by volunteers, or *sewadars*. Each day, the langar feeds 50,000 to 75,000 devotees.

"Our menu is simple: dal, *saag*, *kheer*," said the *sewadar* who took the monks around the kitchen.

And, of course, thousands of chapatis. Large grinders turned 12,000 kgs of wheat into flour each day. There were two kitchens with 11 giant tawas and machines for sieving and kneading dough.

"We have 15 people working on each tawa ... each one does one small part of the job!"

Two ladies were making the *lois* (balls of atta), four of them rolled out the dough, while the rest did *sekne ka kaam*. Making sure each chapati puffed up nicely.

The operation was more efficient, but highly labour-intensive. Luckily, the Golden Temple had volunteers working free of cost.

"We can't afford to employ so many people!" thought Chitranga Chaitanya despondently.

But on festival days, even the volunteers could not keep pace. And at that time, they pressed into service an automatic roti-making machine. The crowning glory of the humble kitchen.

"This machine can produce 5,000 chapatis an hour," said the sewadar with pride.

But the Jaipur kitchen was already feeding 20,000 children a day.

"If we need 50,000 chapatis a day, each machine will need to run for 10 hours!" thought Chitranga Chaitanya.

Buying more than one was out of the question. Each machine occupied 2,000 square feet of space, and the purchase cost was ₹25 lakh.

The monks left the kitchen disheartened. The next morning, their host in Amritsar took them to a small restaurant near the Golden Temple for breakfast.

"*Bhaisaab*," said their host to the owner of the restaurant. "*Chapati banane wali machine ke baare mein aapko kuch pataa hai?*"

Indeed, the restaurant owner was a goldmine of information. He gave the inside story.

"*Machine ki chapati moti banti hai. Khaane mein mazaa nahin aata.*"

The machine was actually designed to make pita bread — not the light and soft chapati eaten in every Indian home. It had been donated to the temple by a devotee from Lebanon.

"*Sabse bada problem aapko bataaon* — when the machine breaks down, they have to fly down the technician from Lebanon."

Now the roti-making machine was looking like a lost cause. Just then, he added, "But Swamiji," he added. "*Main ek shakhs ko jaanta hoon.* He can make the machine for you."

The company was Om Engineering Works in the industrial town of Rajpura, 38 kms from Chandigarh.

Vidya Sagar had inherited the family business of biscuit-manufacturing. But he was looking for new ideas. When a company called Staple Foods in Pune sent an enquiry for a roti-machine, he modified the biscuit-maker and fulfilled the order.

"I have also supplied to Hindustan Lever," beamed Vidya Sagar. "My machines can make 5,000 chapatis an hour."

"That is good," said Chitranga Chaitanya. "But we need a machine that can produce 10,000 an hour!"

Vidya Sagar confidently declared, "I can do that! But it will cost ₹15 lakh."

"First show us your machine!" said Chitranga Chaitanya. Vidya Sagar took them to his workshop and pointed to a dust-filled contraption, the size of a railway engine. After tinkering with it for an hour, he got the machine to crank out something that looked like a chapati.

"We will take it," said the monks. "But we can pay only ₹12 lakh."

They paid ₹2 lakh advance and left Rajpura feeling pretty good. One month passed, then two, then three. But there was no sign of the machine.

"*Bas ho gaya hai … bhej raha hoon!*" Vidya Sagar would assure.

Vyompada was at his wits' end. He decided to search for more suppliers. They located two small companies situated in Bhiwadi on the Delhi–Jaipur highway.

"I have paid an advance to all three fellows. Now all I can do is wait!" Vyompada reported to the head office. The first machine to arrive could make 3,000 chapatis an hour. The chapatis were thin and tasty but the machine was delicate and frequently broke down.

A second machine arrived. It looked very impressive but it just would not work. After repeated attempts to fix it, the company threw up its hands and that was that.

The third machine came from Vidya Sagar's workshop: it

produced 10,000 chapatis an hour. But the chapatis were hard, like biscuits.

"Do something," Ratnangada Govinda pleaded with Vidya Sagar. "Our children refuse to eat this!"

Vidya Sagar had sent one man along with the machine to operate it. With his help, the monks tinkered around until they understood the problem.

"The chapati is getting cooked on both sides but it is not puffing up. That's why it is hard!"

The conveyor belt was modified to include a meshed section that enabled the chapatis to come in contact with an open flame. As they passed over it, the chapatis puffed up with pride. And so did Vidya Sagar — for a job well done!

When Vasundhara Raje inaugurated the new Akshaya Patra facility in Jagatpura, the chapati-making machines occupied pride of place. But the kitchen still employed some manual workers.

The CM, accompanied by Rajashree Birla and Sudha Murty, saw women sitting on the floor, rolling out chapatis. Swept up by emotion, Vasundhara Raje joined them.

"*Aaj main bahut khush hoon*," she said.

Mother India was finally feeding her children at least one square meal.

CHAPTER 11

SHAURYA

Vyompada reached the Vrindavan kitchen early in the morning to find the watchman lying in a pool of blood.

"Hare Krishna — what is happening!"

The watchman was rushed to the hospital and, luckily, he survived. Vyompada was shaken, but the policeman on duty told him not to worry.

"*Swamiji, yeh UP hai. Chhote-mote ladaai-jhagde hote rehte hai.*"

So different from Bangalore and Jaipur. Here there seemed to be no rule of law!

"I am sending Suvyakta Narasimha Dasa to assist you," said Madhu Pandit.

An engineer from M S Ramaiah Institute of Technology, Suvyakta spoke very little Hindi and had no experience of running a kitchen.

As a student, Suvyakta had many questions. Why study? Why work? Why enter the rat race? *What is the purpose of this existence?*

As a monk, Suvyakta had no questions. If I am being sent to Vrindavan, there must be a higher purpose. *I am ready to serve.*

Suvyakta spent three days a week in Jaipur, helping with the kitchen construction, and four days a week in Vrindavan. This meant catching a windowless UP roadways bus every Monday at 5 am. Even in winter, in the biting cold.

One December evening, Vyompada was away in Haridwar, Suvyakta was alone in the Vrindavan kitchen. A security guard came running to inform him, "*Swamiji! Gate par kuch log hain. Kehte hain yeh jagah khaali kar do.*"

Five hefty fellows were standing there with chakus and country-made revolvers.

"This land is ours! You better vacate it," growled their leader.

Suvyakta stood his ground.

"Do you have any proof that this is your land?" he asked firmly.

The men drove away in an Ambassador car. But Suvyakta had an uneasy feeling. Just that morning they had broken a portion of the compound wall to put up grills.

Suvyakta called the contractor.

"There is an emergency — you need to complete the compound wall tonight."

The contractor immediately sent 20 labourers and they started work. But at around 10 pm there was another hungama.

Two policemen arrived in a jeep and lathi-charged the workers.

"*Niklo yahan se!*" they threatened.

"*Par kyun — yeh jagah toh hamari hai,*" Suvyakta intervened.

The policemen insisted they had received a complaint that Akshaya Patra was illegally occupying the property. They wanted Suvyakta to come to the police station. But he refused, for they did not have a warrant.

From Haridwar, Vyompada advised, "Contact the District Magistrate."

He was unreachable. But Vyompada managed to contact Sudhir Srivastava, who had been the District Magistrate until his transfer a week earlier. The DM called the Senior Superintendent of Police (SSP). Within 10 minutes, the Station House Officer (SHO) arrived and took the two police constables away.

The next morning, a local doctor treated the labourers for their injuries. The compound wall was completed without further interference.

"*Maine suna hai jagah khaali karwane ke liye policewaalon ko kisi ne do lakh diye the,*" said the contractor.

Suvyakta shrugged. The local goons must have thought it would be easy to get a mild-mannered swami off the property. They had obviously not read the *Bhagavad Gita* where Arjun is exhorted to pick up arms, all for the cause of Dharma.

The daily battles Vyompada and Suvyakta had to face were more mundane. Any material brought in from Delhi required a road permit. This meant frequent trips to *sarkari* offices.

"Prabhu, I am going to the commercial tax department," said Suvyakta.

"Darshan of Lord Krishna is easier than darshan of the tax officer!" joked Vyompada.

Funds were sent from Bangalore by demand draft (DD), since RTGS and NEFT didn't exist then. The DD would take five days to clear. Suppliers grumbled about payment delays.

One morning, a local vendor walked into Suvyakta's office. He stood in front of the monk, hands on his hips. A holster with a pistol was clearly visible.

"*Kya, Prabhuji — hamara payment release nahin karenge kya!*"

Suvyakta looked at the man calmly and said, "*Maarna hai to maar do. Radha Rani ke baagh mein agar hum apna shareer tyaag dein … hamein badi khushi hogi!*"

Immediately, the man's demeanour changed. He cast his eyes downward and folded his hands.

"*Maaf kijiye, Prabhuji…. Hamara payment release kar dijiye.*"

The man had supplied paver blocks of poor quality. There was an ongoing dispute about the amount to be paid. The matter was settled amicably.

Then there were logistical issues. Unlike Bangalore, Mathura–Vrindavan was a rural area with low population density. Each school had just 60 to 70 students. So, to reach more students, one had to cover more schools. This meant more vans.

"We are using three times the number of vehicles as Bangalore!" exclaimed Vyompada one morning. Naturally, this meant more drivers, guards and helpers.

The weather presents its own challenge. In winter, the day-time temperature is 14 to 15 degrees — keeping the food hot was not easy. In summer, night-time temperatures are 32 to 33 degrees. There is a risk of food spoiling quickly. But the biggest problems came in the rainy season.

"*Swamiji — hamaari gaadi palat gayi hai*," came the frantic call from a driver on a torrential August morning.

A crane was sent to lift the vehicle, while a stand-by was dispatched to the schools on that route. Another time, an Akshaya Patra van got stuck on a narrow road. A tractor was blocking its path, irrigating the fields.

"*Aadha ghanta lagega*," informed the farmer. The driver had no choice but to wait! The school was asked to delay its lunch break by half an hour.

But everyone was not so co-operative. Prior to Akshaya Patra, the mid-day meal scheme was in the hands of the village *pradhans*. Now, they no longer received a cash grant. And they had lost status. Many pradhans were, therefore, unhappy.

One morning, an Akshaya Patra van was blocked by angry villagers. The pradhan said, "Yesterday we found a lizard in the food. We will not allow your vehicle to pass!"

The District Magistrate summoned Vyompada.

"Please … let us investigate the matter and get back to you!" said the monk.

The Akshaya Patra team rushed to the village and asked the pradhan to show the lizard. He opened a tiffin box and triumphantly pulled out a slimy black object.

Closer inspection revealed it was a banana peel that had fallen into the halwa.

Later that evening, Suvyakta sent a photo of the 'lizard' to the head office. It took 25 minutes for the 100 KB file to get uploaded.

"The connection is very slow," sighed Suvyakta.

The process of winning the hearts of people is even slower. It took more than two years for the locals to accept these 'outsiders'.

And then the pradhans came to the Akshaya Patra to say, "*Aap log acchha kaam kar rahe hain. Hamare gaon mein bhi shuru kijye.*"

CHAPTER 12

KARUNA

As Akshaya Patra expanded, there were new and different challenges.

"The commissioner wants us to start the mid-day meal at a school in DJ Halli," said Abhay Jain.

The school in question was a government school with 100% minority community students. DJ Halli is predominantly Muslim and, in police parlance, a 'sensitive' area.

Madhu Pandit hesitated slightly.

"We are happy to start the program, but will there be any objection?"

After all, the food was cooked on the ISKCON temple premises.

"Let us invite the community elders to the temple to have a meal," said Abhay. "Let them see and decide for themselves."

The more orthodox elements refused to come. As it was against their beliefs to step inside a Hindu temple. But a sizable group did visit and sample the food. They went back satisfied — there was nothing 'Hindu' about the program.

"If they want to say *Bismillah* before eating, do you have any problem?" asked T M Vijay Bhaskar, State Commissioner for education.

"No, they are free to say whatever they like," said Madhu Pandit.

Whatever the personal beliefs of the monks, these were not imposed on the children. For the empty stomach of a child knows no caste, creed or religion.

While they worked tirelessly in the kitchen, the other trustees worked quietly, behind the scenes.

"Mohan, donors keep asking if Akshaya Patra has 100% tax exemption," said Madhu Pandit at one of the board meetings.

No matter how noble the cause, a tax benefit made it a more attractive proposition. But 100% exemption under Section 35AC was rarely granted.

"We must do something; we must at least try!" agreed Mohan.

Through the good offices of B Swarup, they secured a meeting with Jaswant Singh, then Finance Minister of India.

In his North Block office, the Finance Minister listened with interest to the work Akshaya Patra was doing. At the end of the brief presentation, Abhay humbly put forth his request.

"Mr Singh, we are seeking tax exemption under 35AC for Akshaya Patra."

The Finance Minister knitted his thick eyebrows.

"You have two kitchens, one in Bangalore, one in Mathura … but tell me, Mr Jain — what about the poorest districts of India? Can you go there?"

Mohan fended the question.

"Well, Mr Singh, to reach those areas we need a different model: a decentralised kitchen."

Jaswant Singh nodded. "Well then, the day you start such a kitchen you will get your 35AC exemption!"

It was a tall order and Akshaya Patra was short on bandwidth. But the following year, when they entered Jaipur, the matter came up again.

"Did you see today's newspaper, Mohan?" asked Abhay.

The headline screamed: '26 tribal children die of malnutrition and hunger.'

The district in question was Baran in Rajasthan, the poorest and most backward in the state. The government had announced 'employment assurance schemes' and Antyodaya Anna Yojana, but it was not enough.

The final push came from Vasundhara Raje herself, "Abhay, we don't know what to do in Baran … *ab aap hi kuch kijiye!*"

A trail of dust followed Ratnangada Govinda's jeep as he made his way to Baran, 300 kms from Jaipur.

"*Aur kitna door hai?*" he asked the driver. The road was dusty, the land sparsely vegetated.

"*Bas aadha ghanta aur,*" assured the driver.

The jeep pulled into a small village with 15 to 20 stone huts. Small children with rickety legs and protruding bellies surrounded the vehicle.

Baran is home to the Sahariya tribe, a nomadic people who were once hunter-gatherers. They lived off the forest and were expert in collecting gum, *tendu* leaf, honey, *mahua* and medicinal herbs.

"*Ab to jungle na rahe aur inko kheti aati nahin,*" explained the driver.

Over the next few days, Ratnangada Govinda learnt the lay of the land. One kitchen with multiple delivery vans was out of the question. Instead, they would have to set up multiple kitchens.

"I can set up a central storehouse in Bhuwagarh — it is a *kasba*, a town. We will employ local women for cooking," proposed Ratnangada Govinda.

"Go ahead," said Chanchalapathi.

A young teacher called Trilok Gautam became an important part of the small team. For he understood the local culture and dialect.

Sahariya women were largely illiterate and hardly stepped out of their homes. So how was one to form a self-help group?

One evening Trilok came back looking quite dejected.

"*Swamiji, jahan bhi jaata hoon auratein mooh chhupa leti hain.*"

As per tradition, the women would not speak to men outside the family. But Ratnangada Govinda found a way to use tradition to his advantage.

"You must always refer to the women as *mataji*. It is a mark of respect."

And sure enough, the matajis agreed to start cooking for the children. Now came the challenge of training them. The women had no concept of 'days of the week' or how to maintain a stock register.

But an even bigger problem was hygiene. People were not in the habit of bathing daily.

"*Ab Surpanakha jaise nakhoon ke saath khana kaise banega!*" wondered Ratnangada Govinda. It was a nightmare for food safety.

Finally, he came up with an idea. Before serving the children, the women were told to offer the food as prasad to a deity.

"*Jo bhi aapke kuldevta hain, aap unko dijiye,*" they were told.

One has to be clean before making any offering to God. And thus the cooks got into the habit of bathing regularly. Ratnangada Govinda heaved a sigh of relief.

But when food delivery started, a new and shocking problem arose. Upper caste children were refusing to touch food cooked by lower caste tribal women. In fact, they did not even want to sit and eat with their *nichle jaati ke* classmates.

It was Mohan who came up with a solution.

"Kids love to play … let them play together!"

He immediately offered to sponsor a football for every school. It was the cheapest sport, a sport which could be played anywhere. And one which required a team.

"It's working!" said Trilok, a few months later. "*Bachche khelne mein itne mast hain, oonch-neech sab bhool gaye.*"

The cooks who did not know how to read or write were now maintaining attendance sheets and cash registers. The program was quickly expanded to cover more schools.

And true to the promise, 100% tax exemption was granted to Akshaya Patra that year.

The decentralised model was later implemented in Mathura district and Nayagarh, in Orissa. When a deadly Naxal attack occurred in the area, only the villages covered by Akshaya Patra were spared.

Was it by accident or by design? Could a simple mid-day meal, served with love and commitment, melt the hardest of hearts?

CHAPTER 13

PRAGATI

In July 2004, ISKCON Hubli organised its first-ever Rath Yatra. It was a procession with a difference.

"There is so much communal tension in our city," said Rajiv Lochana Dasa, President of ISKCON Hubli. "Let us do something to bring the people together."

In the spirit of *sadbhavna*, ISKCON therefore invited leaders of all faiths to join the Rath Yatra. Never before had the city seen *maulvis* pulling the *rath* bearing the deities of Krishna and Balarama. Or Buddhist monks dancing on the street alongside the Hare Krishnas.

The Rath Yatra was a grand success. At the press conference held after the event, a reporter asked, "Swamiji, is there any plan to start Akshaya Patra in Hubli?"

"If Krishna wishes, we will start it," the temple president responded innocently.

The next morning, the local newspaper declared, 'Akshaya Patra to launch in Hubli'. As if it were happening from next week. When Chanchalapathi came to know of this, he was aghast.

"You have made this statement — now what!" he reprimanded the monk. For there was no plan, no land, no vehicle, no money. But Krishna had set something into motion...

Two days later, there was a call from Sudha Murty, Chairperson, Infosys Foundation and wife of Narayana Murthy. Chanchalapathi had interacted with her earlier, when she had expressed a desire to see the Akshaya Patra program in action.

"I would like to contribute in a small way to your worthy cause," she had said, after that visit.

This time, she asked Chanchalapathi, "Swamiji, have you thought about extending the program to the underprivileged children in Hubli? I will support you."

Chanchalapathi was amazed — everything was falling into place. He promised to discuss the idea internally and get back to her.

"We have a commitment for funds," said Madhu Pandit. "Let us start in Hubli immediately!"

Yuddhisthira Krishna Dasa, who was in charge of the temple's prasadam department, was sent to set up the kitchen. Under the guidance of Chitranga Chaitanya Dasa.

They were hunting for a space to take up on rent, when there was another stroke of luck.

Any restaurant bearing the name 'Kamat' cannot be wanting for customers. But this particular Kamat had fallen on bad times. Since the entrance to Hubli station had been shifted, the crowds bypassed the restaurant. It was now empty and forlorn.

The owner of the Kamat restaurant in Hubli was Ganesh Kamat. When he heard that ISKCON was looking for a kitchen, he came forward.

"You can take over these premises," he said. "I won't charge any rent."

Only steam-cooking equipment had to be brought in. Thus, very quickly, the Hubli kitchen could be inaugurated. In July 2004, Akshaya Patra Hubli began feeding 7,500 children. By the end of the school year, the makeshift kitchen was serving over 25,000 meals a day.

"Prabhu, all the schools in Hubli–Dharwad district want Akshaya Patra. But we cannot expand any more in this kitchen!" said a frazzled Yuddhisthira Krishna.

There was barely enough space for three cauldrons of sambar and five cauldrons of rice. Due to the lack of storage space, Yuddhisthira Krishna could not make any bulk purchases.

"We pay more for dals and spices than Bangalore!" he often complained.

The District Commissioner finally allotted a 2.5-acre plot of land to Akshaya Patra Hubli.

"This time we cannot build a kitchen, we must build a mega-kitchen!" declared Madhu Pandit.

Fate had intervened and Mrs Murty had committed the funding from her personal assets towards building of an entire kitchen in the new plot between Hubli and Dharwad.

The goal was to build a facility with the capacity to feed 2 lakh children.

Naturally, this required a very different design, very different thinking.

"It's not that we can just go and copy some other kitchen," mused Madhu Pandit. "The problems we face are unique."

Even as this one-of-a-kind kitchen was being visualised, Yuddhisthira Krishna and his crew moved into the under-construction building. It was chaotic but there was a whole lot of space. By September 2006, this interim old-style kitchen was already feeding 1.15 lakh children.

The Hubli mega-kitchen took more than two years to be completed. Spread over three floors, it looked like an industrial factory and operated like one, as well.

"Madam, we would like to give you a complete tour," said Chitranga Chaitanya to Mrs Murty. Hence, on the day of the inauguration, Mrs Murty arrived early.

The ground floor was for packing and loading operations. Tons of food grains and fresh vegetables arrived every week and underwent quality inspection. But the rice posed a big problem. As per the mid-day meal scheme, the government supplied 100 grams of rice per child per day to Akshaya Patra.

"But see the quality!" said Madhu Pandit, shaking his head in dismay. The rice flowing through his fingers was mixed with rusty nails and stones. The kitchen required 12,000 to 15,000

kgs of rice each day. How could such large quantities
be cleaned manually?

"This is our first innovation — the de-stoning machine,"
said Madhu Pandit proudly. "The vibrating mechanism
removes wood, sand, and any other particles."

The clean rice was sent to a silo on the roof, using
motorised buckets. These silos were similar to the air-tight
containers used in homes.

"Only thing, our containers have sensors to monitor the
food grains."

The action now shifted to the second floor, known as the
pre-preparation area. Each evening, dozens of women wearing
caps and aprons peeled 8,000 to 9,000 kgs of vegetables. The
sabzi was then washed in chlorine water, cut by machines and
kept in cold storage.

"Only tomatoes and coconuts we cut and shred fresh, just
before cooking."

Mrs Murty nodded approvingly. They moved to an area
where rice and dal were being washed. Some of the men were
gesturing to each other vigorously.

"Is this a special code you use in the kitchen?" asked Mrs
Murty.

"Madam, we are employing some deaf people," explained
Chitranga Chaitanya. Sign language was indeed the perfect
way to communicate in a noisy kitchen!

Now came the most interesting part. The cooking area was
situated on the first floor. How to send these tons of dal, rice
and vegetable into cauldrons?

"This is our second innovation: gravity flow," beamed Madhu Pandit. "We use the laws of physics to our advantage."

For example, the sambar would be cooked on the first floor and sent via chutes to the delivery floor below.

On the first floor stood eight cauldrons of 1,200 litres capacity to cook sambar. There were 10 cauldrons to cook rice. All the pots were stirred manually with long steel ladles. Each vat of sambar required 90 minutes of cooking. While 100 kgs of rice would be done in just 15 minutes.

"But where is the gas?" cried Mrs Murty, all of a sudden. For there was no flame beneath any of the cauldrons.

This was the most crucial aspect of the cooking process. No amount of LPG could cook such quantities in five short hours. The secret was high pressure steam sent to the kitchen from the boiler room through a dedicated pipeline.

"The aroma is heavenly," said Mrs Murty as they passed through the kitchen. A quality inspector was standing next to a cauldron with a thermometer.

"His job is to keep checking the temperature. It should be 90 to 98°C to ensure food safety!"

Finally, the piping hot food was sent through special pipes to delivery vessels on the ground floor. A 'tap' regulated the flow of food — just the right amount.

Every vessel had a 'batch id' and moved on a conveyor belt to the loading area.

Insulated vans with spill-proof metallic grids would be standing ready to take the piping hot food to schools in a 40-km radius of the kitchen.

"We start at 4.30 am and the last meal leaves by 8.30 am," said a beaming Chitranga Chaitanya.

Mrs Murty had seen the Bangalore kitchen, but the size and scale at Hubli was something else. Her ₹6 crore donation had been well spent.

"Swamiji, this is fantastic! But the proof is in the pudding. Let me see if food made at this scale still tastes as good," said Mrs Murty, her eyes twinkling.

As she put a spoonful of hot sambar into her mouth, Chitranga Chaitanya's heart thumped faster.

"Aah ... this is better than the sambar we have at home!" exclaimed Mrs Murty with a satisfied smile. "What masala do you use?"

All the standard spices but cooked with the 'right consciousness'.

Satvik food, which satisfies the mind, the body and the soul.

CHAPTER 14

STHAPANA

"My walkie-talkie is dead!" exclaimed Yuddhisthira Krishna one morning.

The new kitchen in Hubli was an engineering marvel. But it was vertical, not horizontal, and poor communication created many a mess. Cooking techniques and recipes had to be modified now and then. The kitchen was thus one giant culinary laboratory. And the 'scientists' were busy at work.

"We must not add coconut to the dal," concluded Yuddhisthira Krishna after dozens of experiments. "The sambar gets spoilt by afternoon."

It was important to know the exact temperature at which to add spices. And how long to boil water for perfectly-cooked rice. This attention to detail made cooking not just an art but a science.

No one was more pleased about this effort than Janardhana

Dasa. A BTech graduate from NIT Trichy, Janardhana
felt strongly about food safety and the need to implement
processes.

Back in 2002, the young monk had attended a two-
day workshop on internal auditing by the DNV-GL, an
international certification and classification body.

"We must implement the HACCP (Hazard Analysis
Critical Control Point) system in our kitchen," he said to
Madhu Pandit and Chanchalapathi.

A team of experts identified where food was most
vulnerable to contamination. Soon after, Akshaya Patra hired
its first quality officer, a recently retired gentleman who was
a food safety expert.

Slowly, Akshaya Patra was acquiring more structure.
A general manager and a finance head had been appointed.
However, one weak link remained.

"We need professional help with marketing," said
Chanchalapathi.

And soon, he would have his wish.

"So, have you ever considered a job in the social sector?"
enquired Abhay.

Rama Prakash was caught off-guard by the question.
A seasoned advertising professional, she was currently enjoying
a break. Having just moved to the Garden City with her

husband and young daughter.

Abhay and Rama were chatting at an ISKCON function in Bangalore.

"Why don't you meet the Vice-Chairman, Chanchalapathi Dasa?" he urged.

"Okay, I will," replied Rama out of politeness.

The meeting took place in the lobby of a hotel on Infantry Road. Rama's young daughter Shruti was running around as the 'job interview' was conducted.

"Mummy, are you going to join a kitchen?" the little girl asked innocently.

It sounded rather funny, when she put it that way. Rama was not very sure.

"Should I work with an NGO? I am not a jeans and *jhola*, do-gooder type!" she thought. No, Rama was as straitlaced as they came.

What's more, this was not client servicing but hardcore sales and marketing.

"All right," said Rama. "Let me give it a shot for six months."

Rama Prakash joined Akshaya Patra as GM, Marketing and Communications.

Actually, there was no department — it was to be set up by her from scratch.

"There is just no system, everything is unorganised!" thought Rama on her first day at work.

The work so far had been handled by Usha Dhanraj and a volunteer named Gita Kulkarni. It was hardly enough!

"Gita, I need eight hours of your time every day. So instead of a volunteer, you become a full-time employee!" said Rama.

The job before this three-person department was to present a one-year plan and a five-year strategy. Plan being short-term and strategy, long-term.

The first thing Rama did was a SWOT (Strengths, Weakness, Opportunity and Threat) analysis. This revealed a startling fact: the bulk of the money was coming in from the trustees.

"We must get more donors," said Rama. "Let us target corporates and HNIs (High Net Worth Individuals)."

The team decided to focus on companies in Bangalore who were part of CII or in the software sector. To target these donors effectively, Rama worked on putting together a database. A more attractive brochure and an annual report.

"You see, an annual report is not just about numbers. We must use it to tell our story."

For example, 93% of the money raised by Akshaya Patra went directly to the mid-day meal. This was a rare feat among NGOs.

"Let us start sending a newsletter to the existing donors." With basic marketing and communication tools in place, the team was ready to hit the road. While Usha and Geeta approached corporates, Rama went after the big fish. She decided to target the mine owners of Bellary.

As luck would have it, Rama personally knew N K Jain, Vice-Chairman at Jindal Steel. So she set up a meeting.

"*Aaj kal kya kar rahi ho*, Rama?" asked Mr Jain.

"Akshaya Patra *ke liye kaam kar rahi hoon*," she answered.

"*Arre wah! Tum log to bahut accha kaam kar rahe ho.* Why don't you start a kitchen at Toranagallu, near our mining plant?"

He invited Rama to come and make a presentation to his HR heads. The deal was sealed at the end of that meeting.

"We will give you five to seven acres of land for the kitchen, ₹2–3 crore for capital expenses and ₹1 crore for the feeding program, year on year."

The last point was a crucial one, which Rama had insisted on. Any corporate who gave a donation would have to sign an MOU for three years or five years.

"That way we can plan our budgets and not do fire-fighting!" she said.

The Bellary kitchen started operations in July 2006 with 50,000 children.

Buoyed by this success, Rama decided to target more mine owners.

"I read in the newspaper that they are making something like ₹4 crore profit every week! Surely they can afford to donate some of it…."

The trick was to understand the psyche of the mine owner. First of all, there was the attraction of 100% tax exemption under Section 35AC. Second — and equally important — was earning brownie points with the government and with workers.

Rama would propose, "Sponsor the program in schools near your mines. Parents will be grateful *ki seth na hamaare liye kuch kiya hai.*"

While such appeals did create interest, a gentle push from an authority figure gave additional momentum. The Police

Commissioner of Bellary, Pankaj Thakur, was known to Rama.
He let her keep 'donor forms' in his office.

Akshaya Patra got a lot of word-of-mouth publicity due to
this.

The toughest part was meeting the decision-maker and
making a pitch. The mine-owning Marwaris did not care much
for corporate etiquette.

"*Accha aap hai Rama? Kya chahiye aapko?* Tell me in five
minutes," said Mrs Modi, standing outside the washroom.

Rama had to be quick-witted and come to the point fast.

When Chanchalapathi learned that Rama had not made
a single PowerPoint presentation in the last two years, he was
aghast.

At the same time, Akshaya Patra was reaching out to high-
profile journalists, CEOs and HR heads. It was not enough to
just say 'we are feeding children'.

"Show us what the impact of your program is," they said.

The best way to convince these folks was to conduct 'market
research'.

"Let us hire A C Nielsen and Co to do a qualitative study,"
Rama proposed.

The A C Nielsen report highlighted the positive impact
of Akshaya Patra on education outcomes. The meal was 'more
than a meal'. It was an incentive to come to school, to stay in
school and study better.

Later that year, Harvard Business School published a case study on Akshaya Patra. Catapulting the organisation onto a global stage. Translating the language of poverty into the language of business.

For hunger is rarely understood by those with the fortune of a full stomach.

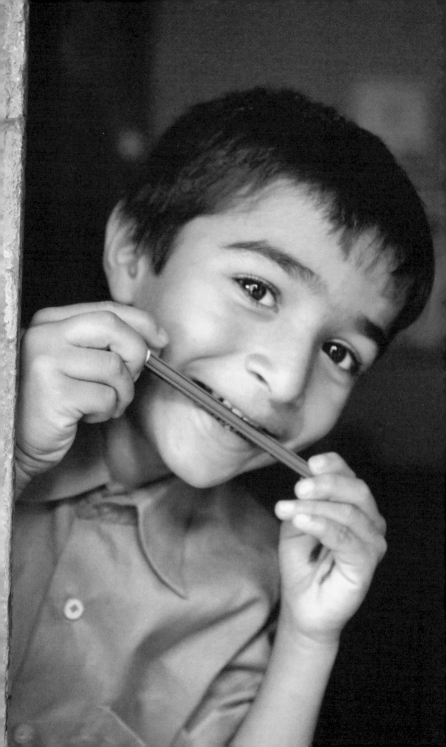

CHAPTER 15

KALPAVRIKSHA

On a crisp morning in December, two monks walked down East 57th Street in Manhattan. The coats they wore over their thin dhotis were not doing a very good job.

"It's colder than I remember from my last visit," said Chanchalapathi. His companion nodded.

It wasn't just the temperature. The monks missed the warmth of living in ISKCON temples on their travels. For the last five years, ISKCON Bangalore had been fighting a case against the ISKCON governing body in Mayapur. They were not welcome anywhere.

Hence, the monks were staying with Ravi Narayan, a devotee from Bangalore now living in the US. He had arranged interactions with the local Kannada Sangha and meetings with some doctors.

"Prabhu, I thought these NRIs would contribute

generously," said Chitranga Chaitanya. The response so far had been disappointing.

As they passed by an Indian grocery store, the monks decided to try their luck. Perhaps the owner would make a small donation.

"Hare Krishna!" said Chanchalapathi cheerfully. A harassed-looking Gujarati man looked up from the cash register. Before they could say anything about Akshaya Patra, he started ranting.

"So you are here with your begging bowl.... Listen to me, this is not India. *Wahan yeh sab chalta hai, yahan nahin!*"

The monks were stunned by this rude outburst. They left without a word.

"Don't be upset," said Chanchalapathi to his companion. "Remember how Srila Prabhupada came to America with $8 in his pocket? He must have gone through much worse!"

Prabhupada used to sit under a tree in Washington Square Park chanting the Hare Krishna mantra.

Gradually, he attracted a bunch of followers. And established the first ISKCON temple, where he cooked for devotees with his own hands.

"You are right," said Chitranga Chaitanya. "Prabhupada is our inspiration. There must be a better way to collect donations for Akshaya Patra ... we just need to find it!"

There is an old jungle saying, you never find the Phantom, he finds you. Something like that happened when Chitranga Chaitanya met Gururaj 'Desh' Deshpande at his Boston home.

The handsome, mild-mannered NRI looked no different from so many other Indian-Americans. But beneath the soft exterior lay a hard-boiled, super-successful, serial entrepreneur.

"Swamiji, the work Akshaya Patra is doing is fantastic. I would like to help you."

On that first meeting, Desh pulled out his cheque book and gave a donation.

During his next visit to India, Desh agreed to support the expansion of the Hubli kitchen. With a generous personal contribution. But he also went a step further.

"Let us create a fundraising organisation in the US. I have office space and I will employ one or two people to make it happen."

It was a radical new idea. The trustees raised doubts and concerns.

"Won't fundraising cost money?" said Mohan. "That money could be used to feed more children!"

Until then, ₹94 out of every ₹100 raised by Akshaya Patra was used for meals. The administration and operating cost of the organisation was extremely low. Because it was mainly run by volunteers.

Desh had a different perspective. He was on the board of MIT (Massachusetts Institute of Technology), a private university which had created an $8 billion corpus.

This was possible only because MIT had created a

professional fundraising organisation. It took 150 people working full-time to raise $300-400 million a year.

"You have to invest in marketing, in communication. It costs money to raise money," said Desh.

As an entrepreneur, Desh strongly believed that an organisation should be self-sufficient. It should not be dependent on a few big donors. He offered his own office space as well as $100,000 per annum, to set up a professional fund-raising organisation in the US. The same could be established in Bangalore, to raise funds in India.

After a lot of debate and dialogue, Mohan and Abhay accepted the merit of this idea.

"But on one condition. We should not spend more than ₹15 to raise ₹100. We should never lose our focus on feeding the children!"

"Agreed!" said Desh. "That is why we are all here."

Now came the task of identifying the right people to work with Akshaya Patra in this new avatar.

The initial attempts to hire a professional failed. The culture of Akshaya Patra was very different from that of a corporate.

One employee was a chain-smoker but felt guilty lighting up in his office.

"Oh, that is why we see him drive out of the temple every 15 minutes!" observed Chanchalapathi. Shortly after, the poor man left Akshaya Patra.

It was then that Madhu Pandit proposed the name of Shridhar Venkat, a marketing man and an ISKCON devotee. An electrical engineer and an MBA, Shridhar had been a volunteer for many years. Then, Madhu Pandit invited him to do something bigger.

"Shridhar, why are you building empires for others? Build for Krishna. Build for his children," said Madhu Pandit.

It was a turning point in Shridhar's life, and for Akshaya Patra.

The young professional's initial assignment was with India Heritage Foundation, an ISKCON trust that markets CDs and incense sticks. Bringing income to the temple.

"With your expertise, we can increase our sales manifold," said Madhu Pandit.

While Shridhar Venkat was inspired by Srila Prabhupada, he was a regular householder. With a family, and bills to pay. Unlike the monks, he received a salary.

"We can't match your salary in a multinational job," said Madhu Pandit. "But we will take good care of you."

For the first 18 months, Shridhar received his pay cheque from India Heritage Foundation. But he was also helping Akshaya Patra in many ways, big and small.

It was time to formalise the association.

"I propose that we appoint Shridhar as Executive Director of Akshaya Patra," said Madhu Pandit.

While the board liked his credentials, there was one major stumbling block. The India Heritage Foundation paid Shridhar ₹3 lakh a month. This was a very large sum for a non-profit like Akshaya Patra. And it became a heated point of contention.

"Can we afford to pay this kind of salary?" said Mohan.

"Will paid employees work with the same dedication and spirit of service?"

It was the spiritualist who wore the capitalist hat and pushed the appointment through.

"If Akshaya Patra cannot pay for Shridhar, my temple will continue to pay his salary!" declared Madhu Pandit.

Under these peculiar circumstances, Shridhar joined the organisation to lead the fundraising effort in India.

In Boston, Massachusetts, 13,000 kms away, Desh had just found a CEO for Akshaya Patra USA. It was an accomplished lady, a family friend.

"Madhu, what are your plans now?" Desh asked the lady at the lunch to celebrate his son's graduation from MIT.

"Just reading, listening to music," replied Madhu Sridhar. She had just completed a four-year term as President of the League of Women Voters in Massachusetts.

Madhu had years of experience, both with the corporate and non-profit sector. She had raised over $40 million for the Andover school system in her home state.

"Madhu — you know about Akshaya Patra. I want you to join as CEO."

While Madhu had attended a presentation at the Deshpande home and been convinced enough about the idea to donate, this was a completely different commitment. The organisations she had worked with before had been well-established. Whereas Akshaya Patra was unknown in America.

Then, a voice from within whispered. "You have worked for so many non-profits but you have never worked for India. This is your chance!"

In two opposite corners of the world, a new era for Akshaya Patra had begun.

Some measure progress by what they own, others measure it by what they give. Of their time, their money, their expertise.

For when you take, it is never enough. But the more you give, the more you receive.

CHAPTER 16

PARIKSHA

"Prabhu, main dekh raha hoon … teen din se aap kuch kha nahin rahe hain?"

Achyutha Krishna was startled. This young boy, practically a stranger, was asking such a difficult question.

"I am fasting," mumbled the monk to his companion. How could he tell Mahesh that he had run out of money? The ₹10,000 Achyutha Krishna had brought from Bangalore was exhausted.

"Account opening will take another two-three days," the bank manager had said.

Until then Achyutha Krishna would have to fend for himself in a strange new town where he did not know a soul. Thank God for this boy Mahesh.

"Mere bhai ka Infosys mein jaan-pehchaan hai. To unhone bola aapko kuch madad chahiye…"

Indeed, there was a huge task ahead of Achyutha Krishna in the holy city of Jagannath Puri.

Dr Mona Sharma, Secretary for Women and Child Development, Government of Orissa, had visited the Akshaya Patra kitchen in Bangalore. A meeting with Chief Minister Naveen Patnaik quickly followed. A decision was taken to start a kitchen in Orissa.

"Achyutha Prabhu, you have experience with the Bangalore kitchen," said Madhu Pandit. "The Lord is calling you to his side ... to spread this work."

That night, Achyutha Krishna slept fitfully. How would this new place be? How would he manage alone? As a boy, he had lived with a loving family. As a monk, he had lived in a community. The fatherly presence of Madhu Pandit and Chanchalapathi was always comforting.

"Now I know what it feels like *shaadi ke baad ...*" he thought. Except that as a monk, he was married to a cause. And the love of Krishna would sustain him.

"Prabhu *mujhe samajh nahin aata*," exclaimed Mahesh. "If Lord Krishna loves us, why does he put so many obstacles in our path?"

For despite the CM and top IAS officers blessing the mid-day meal project, there were hurdles every step of the way.

Achyutha Krishna smiled. A devotee may say he has surrendered, but the Lord puts him to the test.

"Krishna wants to see how much risk you will take for him ... how much faith you have!"

That morning, the owner of the cheap guesthouse where

Achyutha Krishna was staying had threatened, "*Paisa nahin hai to niklo yahan se!*"

Yet, Achyutha Krishna calmly went about his business for the day.

That evening, a local businessman came and offered a donation of ₹5,000. He also offered to donate a vehicle to the kitchen.

Achyutha Krishna had passed yet another test.

Orissa is one of the poorest states of India, hence it attracts many NGOs. So much so that 'NGO' has become a code word for running a shady business. For every one person who was helpful and sincere, there was one who wanted some 'benefit'.

"I want to meet and discuss with Mr Akshaya Patra," was the constant refrain.

Achyutha Krishna was baffled until Mahesh explained that 'Patra' is a common surname in Orissa. There are many businessmen with this name. Hence, people had concluded that Akshaya Patra was a businessman who was setting up an NGO to convert his black money to white.

"*Unko bhi usme se kuch cut chahiye.*"

Even after explaining the work of Akshaya Patra and showing people the kitchen facility, there would be scepticism. Why are these non-Oriya people doing something for us? Surely there must be some ulterior motive.

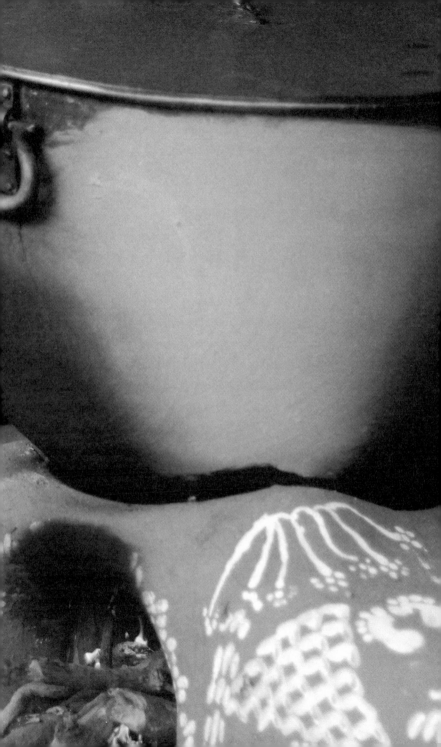

"In Bangalore, I used to feel proud that I am a volunteer with an NGO," remarked Achyutha Krishna sadly. "Over here, they think I am a cheat!"

The Puri kitchen was set up in a government building which had once been a women's college. The feeding program started with 1,000 children in two government schools.

Very soon, Achyutha Krishna realised that kitchen *banana easy hai, chalana mushkil hai*. The reason was that the labour force was extremely unreliable.

"Mahesh, in our kitchens we have some Oriya workers. We have no complaints. But here in Orissa, they just don't want to work!"

During the harvest season, this problem became acute. Every other day, half the workers would fail to turn up. At 7.30 pm, when the preparation work started, there would be a crisis.

At such times, Mahesh would get into a vehicle and drive to a nearby village. He would round up a dozen able-bodied men and bring them back to the kitchen. Along with extra pay for the regular workers, the meal would somehow be cooked and dispatched.

At other times, there were issues with suppliers. Funds from the head office were delayed, hence traders would have to extend credit. Once again, Mahesh would come to their rescue.

"*Main unse baat karta hoon — aap chinta na karo*," he would say to Achyutha Krishna.

The rough and tough young man who was once a local dada and the son of a rich landlord, was becoming emotionally and spiritually mature.

"*Prabhulog se mujhe bahut kuch seekhne ko mil raha hai…. Ab mere saamne kitna bhi bada kaam aaye, woh main kar sakta hoon.*"

Mahesh eventually shut down his computer business and became a full-time volunteer with Akshaya Patra. And what Mahesh lacked in education and experience he made up with his spirit.

"We can purchase talent, we cannot purchase faith," Achyutha Krishna would often say when recruiting kitchen supervisors and department heads.

With the support of faithful staff like Mahesh, Achyutha Krishna took a bold new step. He decided to take Akshaya Patra into the Naxalite-infested district of Nayagarh. Situated 100 kms from Bhubaneshwar, Nayagarh was a low-lying area with dense forest cover. There were very few *pucca* roads in the area. A centralised kitchen would just not work.

Achyutha Krishna visited the Baran kitchen in Rajasthan to understand their model. One advantage Orissa had over Baran was that numerous Self Help Groups, or SHGs, already existed.

"Let us talk to the gram panchayats and ask them to recommend women who can do the cooking."

Grain, oil and spices were provided in a tin box from the central storehouse every 15 days. While vegetables or milk were procured by the women locally, and paid for by Akshaya Patra. But how to ensure that the meals were actually cooked and delivered?

"It is difficult for us to manage one kitchen," said Achyutha Krishna. "How will we monitor 100 kitchens?

Akshaya Patra had its own inspection teams making surprise checks. But even more effective were committees formed with the parents.

"*Aisa lagta hai gaon mein 3G nahin, 10G hai,*" Mahesh reported. It was easy for the villagers to spot when one didi siphoned off a few kilos of rice. The code of the community kept such cheating under control.

An entrepreneur must boldly go where no one has gone before. So it was with the young monks who were deputed to start kitchens.

A management cadre was slowly emerging. Making best use of money and manpower — becoming leaders of men.

CHAPTER 17

SANKATA

One night, at 11 pm, Abhay received a call from Narendra Modi, then Chief Minister of Gujarat.

"Maine aapki sanstha ke baare mein bahut suna hai…" he said.

Modi met the Akshaya Patra team at his official residence, and spent more than two hours with them — mostly listening. A simple vegetarian lunch was served.

Modi remarked, "You should start in Dwarka. Because that is Krishna's place."

Madhu Pandit and Chanchalapathi thought it was a great idea. But after the meeting, Mohan expressed a contrary opinion.

"Swamiji, it is better to start in the capital city, which has the ministers and bureaucrats. Everyone will get sensitised. As a next step, you should do it in Dwarka."

The monks saw the practical merit in this suggestion. The feeding program was therefore launched from Gandhinagar.

A young monk with some experience of running the Vrindavan kitchen was deputed to set up the operation. Jaganmohan Dasa quickly proved his worth.

He rented industrial sheds in the GIDC area to put together a temporary kitchen.

"Shall we begin with 500 or 1,000 children?" asked Jaganmohan. For that was the usual modus operandi when entering a new state.

But this time, caution was thrown to the winds.

"Don't worry," said the administration. "People in Gujarat are charitable, they will come forward and support. You must think big."

Swayed by this promise, the Gandhinagar kitchen launched with a big bang. On the very first day, meals were served to 65,000 students.

This was done with the help of 25 vehicles and 250 workers — cooks, drivers and helpers.

It was an extraordinary achievement but it also put an extraordinary burden on Akshaya Patra.

In Bangalore, alarm bells were ringing in the finance department. A storm had been brewing for some time. Now, the consequences would start pouring down.

"There is no money … no money at all!" said T S Ramaswamy, Director of Finance. He had been with Akshaya Patra since its inception, and seen many ups and downs.

But nothing as dire as this.

To be sure, there were occasional shortfalls. Then there would be a 10-day Dusshehra break or summer holidays and, in that time, funds would come from somewhere.

But in October 2007, outstandings stood at ₹5 crore and donations could not keep pace.

"How could we let this happen?" said Siva Sudhir, shaking his head in dismay.

The young CA had recently quit his job with a 'Big Four' accounting firm and joined the organisation. He was tired of manipulating balance sheets and telling white lies.

But the truth behind Akshaya Patra's finances was a bitter pill to swallow.

With every good intention, the feeding program had grown rapidly. In the last one year, state-of-the-art kitchens had been built in Jaipur, Vrindavan, Hubli and Bangalore.

"We have used the money meant for day-to-day expenses to buy land and equipment," explained Ramaswamy.

Meanwhile, the number of mid-day meals had crossed 4 lakh per day. The gap grew wider each day, with outstandings of more than ₹5 crore with vendors.

Trustee Ramadas Kamath put in valiant efforts to boost the inflow of funds. He organised a benefit concert with singer Sonu Nigam and some corporate events.

"It is too little, too late," said Ramaswamy at the board

meeting in October 2007.

The trustees silently contemplated the future. But one thing was certain. The feeding program for children could not stop — at any cost.

Finally, Mohan conceded there was only one option.

"We will have to take a short-term loan," he said.

Siva Sudhir could not believe his ears. It was sheer madness to take a loan to do charity work. How in the world would the money be paid back?

Against every accounting norm, the board gave the green signal. Through their good offices, Ramadas Kamath and V Balakrishnan arranged a ₹1 crore overdraft from State Bank of India, Mysore.

The bank also extended a ₹50 lakh line of credit to help tide over the working capital crunch.

The trustees put on a brave face, but privately they were worried. How would this loan get paid off?

A couple of months later, Sudha Murty bumped into Ramadas at Infosys. In fact, she rarely visited this particular campus.

"Why such a long face Ramadas? Everything okay?" she asked kindly.

"Madam, there are no funds in Akshaya Patra," replied Ramadas. He related the sorry state they were in. "Soon, we may have to stop the program!"

Akshaya Patra was close to Mrs Murty's heart. She had visited schools, eaten with the children, seen their happy smiles after the meal.

"Oh … we can't allow such a thing to happen!"

The next day a generous cheque from the Infosys Foundation arrived in the name of Akshaya Patra.

To Madhu Pandit and Chanchalapathi, it was divine providence. But for Mohan and Abhay, this was a wake-up call.

Today they had survived, but only by the skin of their teeth.

The trustees took some crucial decisions. In future, revenue expenditure and capital expenditure would be two separate and watertight compartments.

"We will build new kitchens only when a donor commits the funds required for that purpose," said Ramadas Kamath.

These decisions would bear fruit in the years to come. But for a period of six months, Akshaya Patra continued to hang by a thread.

Chanchalapathi called up all his kitchen heads and gave a terse directive.

"Don't ask the head office for money. We have no money … you are on your own!"

In Vrindavan, a stunned Suvyakta put the receiver down. His kitchen was already struggling — it was a rural area, with no local donors.

What's more, they were feeding over 1 lakh children each day.

"Even with this new chapati machine, it's impossible to keep up!"

The machine could produce 10,000 chapatis an hour, but the requirement was 2 lakh chapatis. Even with 40 women to supplement the effort, it was a daily struggle.

Ideally, they needed more and better machines. Now, there was zero budget for R & D, and there was a crunch from all sides.

"The price of dal is going through the roof!" worried Suvyakta.

Common sense decreed the use of cheap substitutes. But at Akshaya Patra, cutting the nutritional content of meals was *not* an option.

It is in man's darkest hour that he sees the light. The trouble at Akshaya Patra was one such moment in time.

For necessity is the mother of invention, and desperation, its father. The womb of creation was pregnant with possibility. Ideas waiting to be born.

CHAPTER 18

AVISHKARA

"Prabhu, we can make so many improvements to our kitchen!" Prahaladisha Dasa had recently joined the Vrindavan kitchen as Operations Manager. And he was itching to 'do something'.

An electronics engineer from M V Jayaraman College, Prahaladisha had a childlike enthusiasm for his work. And a knack of identifying problems.

Soon after joining, he made it his habit to visit schools and talk to children. In the process, he discovered the problem of 'sticky rice'.

"*Humein chipku chawal pasand nahin hai,*" complained the children.

For in south India, where rice is eaten with sambar, sticky is the norm. But in the north, they like it long and fluffy. Each grain separate from the other.

The problem was that, no matter what they tried, the rice

would form lumps.

In a eureka moment, Prahaladisha realised that the answer lay in the grain itself.

"We have some broken rice, some whole rice. Broken rice cooks faster, it clumps!"

The solution was simple: use only whole grain *basmati* rice. But that was a luxury the kitchen could ill-afford.

The rice supplied by FCI had a mix of broken and whole grain. But the sorting machine in the kitchen could not distinguish between the two.

"What we need is a machine that can separate rice based on its length," thought Prahaladisha. But no one knew *where* to find such a machine.

So the young monk embarked on a quest. With one driver and one vehicle.

"I will not return home until I have found this machine," he declared.

Vrindavan is in UP but close to Rajasthan as well as Haryana. Prahaladisha scoured all three states. Finally, with the help of an ISKCON devotee, he found it.

Agrosaw, a company in Ambala, was selling the exact machine they needed.

"We can use the long rice for *pulao* and the short rice for khichdi," said Prahaladisha with a sigh of satisfaction.

But now, there was a new and pressing issue. The price of dal had skyrocketed while the head office was reeling under a financial crisis.

Prahaladisha had a new problem to urgently solve.

This time, the monk went to the mandis and learnt everything there was to learn about lentils. He soon realised there was a complex supply chain.

The farmer is separated from the buyer by three or four middlemen. What's more, these chaps add artificial colour and cheap oil to the dal to make it 'look good'.

"We must buy unpolished dal directly from the farmer," decided Prahaladisha. This would not only be cheaper, but healthier.

So Prahaladisha once again took off in a car, visiting mandi after mandi. To find the best quality lentils at the best possible price.

As Prahaladisha interacted with farmers, he picked up their lingo. At Badarpur, he finally met a vendor who was willing to supply unpolished dal.

But when he asked for *moong* dal, the vendor showed them *moth* dal.

"This is not moong dal," Prahaladisha exclaimed. "You are giving us a cheaper variety and charging us more for it!"

The vendor was shocked. "How did you know?" he asked.

He realised the buyer was no fool. And could not be cheated. A deal was struck and the 'dal crisis' was permanently solved.

But there was to be no rest for Prahaladisha. For he was now eyeing a problem of epic proportions. The problem of chapati production.

"A daily headache for our kitchen!" the supervisors would grumble.

As per government norms, Akshaya Patra was to supply 100 gms of wheat per child (or two chapatis). 1 lakh children therefore required 2 lakh chapatis.

"Even with our machine, we cannot meet the demand!"

The capacity of the roti-making machine was only 10,000 pieces an hour. The kitchen employed 40 women, mostly widows, to supplement the effort.

But on most days, the quantity fell short.

"Prahaladisha, the head office can't send us more funds, but we need a faster machine!" said Suvyakta.

Designing such a machine required experimentation. These experiments required equipment like variable speed motors and temperature controls.

"What I need is a full-fledged R & D lab," thought Prahaladisha despondently. But he was not one to give up so easily....

Prahaladisha decided to break down the big problem into several small problems.

For example: what was the optimal width of the machine? A wider machine could be used to cook more chapatis in the same amount of time.

But experiments with a wider machine were a failure. The chapatis in the centre got burnt while the ones on the side remained undercooked.

The roti machine supplier told Prahaladisha, "It's an impossible task!"

At an international food and hospitality exhibition in New Delhi, Prahaladisha chanced upon a stall by a firm in Holland. They were making 'continuous baking' machines with cutting-edge technology.

"I am looking to build a machine that bakes 40,000 chapatis per hour," said Prahaladisha to the Dutch man managing the stall.

"Really?" he replied in amusement.

"Yes … we already have a machine that cooks 10,000 chapatis an hour."

The man was stunned.

"Impossible!" he snapped. "Such a machine cannot be made in India!"

As Prahaladisha explained how the machine worked, the man grew more curious. They moved to a meeting room to discuss the design issues the monk was facing.

The hours passed, but neither technologist noticed the time. When they finally finished, the Dutch man was in for a rude shock. All the visitors had left!

"What am I going to do? I don't even remember the name of my hotel!" the Dutch man cried in panic.

"Don't worry. I will make sure you reach safely," comforted Prahaladisha.

He took the foreigner from one 5-star hotel to another. Finally, the Dutch man recognised the one he was staying in.

Kindness is a bridge between people and cultures. The Dutch man now saw Prahaladisha as a friend — and an equal.

"I want to help you build this machine. I will conduct experiments in my lab and send you the results," he promised.

This work was done as a personal project. At the risk of losing his job. This informal collaboration helped Prahaladisha immensely. Helping him to 'crack' many a problem and boosting his confidence.

But all the pieces of the puzzle were yet to be found. Prahaladisha visited several biscuit factories to observe their methods.

Normally an industrial facility would not allow outsiders, but with a monk in saffron dress, managers let down their guard.

Little did they know that Swamiji was keenly observing the die-cutting machines and alignment of the conveyor belt.

"At each factory I am able to get one or two good ideas!" said Prahaladisha.

Over a period of eight months, he was able to solve the 30 to 40 small problems with the existing machine. Armed with this knowledge, Prahaladisha went to meet Vidya Sagar, the man whose company was supplying the roti-making machines.

The monk explained the improvements he sought in intricate detail. Vidya Sagar was astounded.

"*Aapko to andar ki har baat pata hai,*" he said.

Vidya Sagar's methods of working were unique. The

blueprint of his machine was not on paper. It was only imprinted in his mind.

What's more, no machine was built on exact measurements. It was proportionate: if the first roller is 1, then the second must be 1.4 times, and so on. There was therefore no problem in going to scale.

Earlier, Vidya Sagar thought Akshaya Patra was simply a client asking for crazy numbers. That perception had changed.

"*Ab mujhe aap par bharosa hai!*" he said.

The final question was, how much would it cost? The 10,000-chapati machine cost ₹12 lakh. Logically, a machine with four times the capacity would cost four times as much.

Luckily, the Vrindavan kitchen had received a donation of ₹45 lakh from Japan.

The heads of the Ahmedabad, Jaipur and Vrindavan kitchens gathered to make the crucial phone call. And negotiate the price.

Vidya Sagar heard them out and promised to call back in half an hour.

The monks waited with bated breath.

The phone rang and Vidya Sagar gave his quotation.

"According to my calculations, the new machine will cost ₹15 lakh," he said.

The monks could not believe their ears. On the spot, they placed an order for three machines.

Six months later, the first 40,000 rotis-per-hour machine arrived in Vrindavan. Such was Vidya Sagar's confidence that he did not conduct any trial run.

When the first chapatis rolled off the conveyor belt, he was proved right.

Prahaladisha came to be known as the 'Edison' of Akshaya Patra. For genius is 1% inspiration and 99% perspiration.

One and all must perspire. So that children can aspire. For a better, brighter, future.

JNANA
YOGA

Knowledge leads to excellence
(2009 – 2016)

CHAPTER 19

PRAYATNA

In the V K Hill kitchen in Bangalore, Vamshidhara Dasa had spent yet another day sweating over the boiler machine.

Although the automated kitchen was just four years old, it was not functioning properly. The maintenance of machines was poor.

"In last 60 days we have had a breakdown on 55 days!" said Vamshidhara.

An electronics engineer and former employee of IBM, Vamshidhara had set up the Vizag kitchen from scratch. His technical brain was not happy with just fire-fighting.

"We need to understand the root cause of the problem."

This led to the creation of schedules and maintenance sheets. Key parts that broke down frequently were identified. Spares were procured and kept on-site.

A back-up plan was put in place, with extra machines on

stand-by.

While technical issues could be handled in-house, there were issues on the commercial side. A well-wisher from Kolkata stepped in to help.

Ravindra Chamaria first heard about the mid-day meal program at a TIE conference in USA. A visit to the Hubli kitchen convinced him to become a patron.

Chamaria had done a variety of businesses, from running a jute factory to trading in Russia. He brought to Akshaya Patra not only money, but commercial acumen.

"To save money we need to buy material in bulk and pay in cash," he advised.

A Central Strategic Sourcing committee was put in place with Chamaria as advisor. Various kitchens were encouraged to share best practices.

"We are using unpolished tur dal with good results, let us use the same in all our kitchens," said Suvyakta.

This one measure alone would save Akshaya Patra ₹1 crore in the next one year.

The kitchens used to buy oil in tins. But it was much cheaper to purchase by the tanker. To store the oil, large vats were built in each location.

Similarly, it was better to go to the source of origin to buy the best raw material. Thus *aloo* was sourced in bulk from Agra, while A1 *jeera* was available in Unjha in Gujarat.

"We can keep dry items in cold storage instead of buying them weekly," said Chamaria.

The making of tomato puree was outsourced to Mysore

Fruits, Bangalore, due to lower costs.

Every rupee saved meant a meal for a few more children. And that made the effort worth it.

Another source of stress was the dependence of all the kitchens on Bangalore for funds.

"Jaipur has so many wealthy traders and jewellers but we are not able to get donations," observed Chanchalapathi.

Ravindra Chamaria offered to help Akshaya Patra reach out to the Marwari community. He had a name and a network, but most importantly, he understood their psyche.

To get a Marwari to open his purse-strings, you need to appeal to his sense of pride.

"Why should children from Rajasthan take donations from south India?" Chamaria asked the who's who of Jaipur.

The second thing he did was present a strong business case. For a Marwari is most comfortable when the 'calculations' make sense.

"If you give ₹1 to Akshaya Patra, it becomes ₹2!" declared Chamaria.

How was this possible? Because Akshaya Patra and the government share the cost of a mid-day meal 50:50. What's more, the cost of an Akshaya Patra meal is just ₹6. This is possible due to the use of technology and the scale of operations. So each rupee goes much further.

"Come with me to our kitchen and see for yourself," Chamaria said. This was what finally convinced the hard-boiled businessmen *ki yeh koi kahaani nahin, sach hai.*

A regional committee was formed in each city where Akshaya Patra was operating. With community leaders at the helm. The goal was to raise local donations.

Indeed, when the Guwahati kitchen was inaugurated, the businessmen of that city came forward to bear the entire running cost.

There was one more aspect of localisation, and that was the menu.

"We must give children nutritious food, but it has to be tasty!" Chanchalapathi often said. But the definition of 'tasty' differed vastly from one state to the other.

The whole of north India does not eat the same kind of chapati. There is a Punjab-style chapati (with no salt), a UP-style chapati (thicker) and a Gujarat-style chapati (paper-thin). There were also distinctive local dishes.

"Our children relish *dal-dhokli*," said Jaganmohan, head of the Ahmedabad kitchen.

In Gujarat, Akshaya Patra also provided fortified *sukhdi* (a sweet made from wheat) to address the issue of iron deficiency. A special sukhdi-making machine had to be improvised in this kitchen.

Similarly, in Orissa, a favourite food item was *dalma* — a thick dal with vegetables. To provide more nutrition, *paneer* was often added.

Back in Bangalore, the children had complaints: "The food

is same-same, it is boring".

So Vamshidhara and his team sat down and invented a new range of 25 sambars. With innovative combos of spices and vegetables.

"Now we have Kerala sambar, Coimbatore sambar, Andhra sambar!"

The best tasting sambars got special names such as '*Krishnamrita sambar*'.

The menu was much-liked by the children and by grown-ups. Mrs Murty was one of them. If work took her near the Akshaya Patra kitchen she would happily drop in and have the mid-day meal with relish.

One day a young man called Rishi Sunak came to the Murthy home. He was Akshata Murthy's fiancé and it was his first trip to India.

Despite Mrs Murty's hectic schedule, she wanted to show him something unique to Bangalore. So she decided to take him for a special meal.

Right in time for lunch, Rishi shared his first meal with his future mother-in-law, not in a fancy restaurant, but in the Akshaya Patra kitchen.

Simple, gracious, auspicious. And memorable.

For every *rajasik* soul, there exists a *tamasik* counterpart.
In mythology, these were the *asuras* — powerful beings with
demonic qualities. In the modern world, we know them as
netas.

Churning the ocean of welfare for notes and votes.

CHAPTER 20

RAJANITI

Chanchalapathi and Janardhana stood in front of the dilapidated building. The structure was completely overgrown with vines and creepers.

"*Idhar dairy lagane ka plan tha,*" said the officer who had accompanied them. But like umpteen government projects, it never took off.

The '*bhoot bangla*' was being offered to Akshaya Patra to set up a kitchen.

"*Yahan koi aata-jaata nahin hai,*" added the officer, helpfully. "*Kehte hain andar saanp hai.*"

Janardhana sighed. He had been shifted from the Jaipur kitchen to start the feeding program in Chhattisgarh. Every new kitchen threw up a fresh set of challenges.

One month earlier, the Steel Secretary had visited the Bangalore kitchen and was very impressed. He spoke to the

Chairman of SAIL (Steel Authority of India Ltd.). Soon after, Madhu Pandit received a call from Delhi. It was Abhijit Mukherjee, Deputy General Manager for Corporate Social Responsibility at the steel giant.

"We wish to fund Akshaya Patra's feeding program," he said. "But you must start kitchens where our steel plants are located."

An MOU was quickly signed between Akshaya Patra and SAIL. The PSU had plants in many different locations. Akshaya Patra chose to start the first kitchen in Bhilai.

Now the hunt was on for a suitable place to set up operations.

"This building will do," said Chanchalapathi confidently. With scrubbing, painting, construction and equipment, the forlorn site transformed into a spanking new kitchen.

No snakes were ever found in the building. But other, more dangerous, snakes were lurking....

The Akshaya Patra kitchen in Bhilai was ready to start feeding 25,000 children. What remained were some routine government permissions.

When Janardhana called on Chief Minister Raman Singh, he was received cordially. "Wonderful program," said the CM. "I am very happy you are doing this."

With the CM's blessing, Janardhana made the necessary

applications and waited for the green signal. He had no clue what storm was brewing.

Bhilai steel city is in district Durg, 50 kms from the capital city. The local politician was not at all pleased. The mid-day meal was his fiefdom and a steady source of income. He leaned on the District Magistrate to deny permission.

When Janardhana went to meet him, he did not say anything directly. But he conveyed a message through one of his *chelas*.

"I pocket ₹5 lakh per month from the mid-day meal scheme. What will you give me?"

Janardhana was willing to call the *neta* to inaugurate the program.

"You will earn goodwill with children and parents. You will get votes in the next election."

The man refused to budge. Janardhana sought a second appointment with the CM.

Raman Singh was once again courteous.

"Please be patient … I will sort it out," he said.

Janardhana continued to follow up with various bureaucrats. They advised him to wait until after the elections. The kitchen was ready, vehicles were standing by. Cooks, drivers and helpers had been hired. But nothing was happening. The SAIL management was putting pressure.

"We have given you the funds — when will you start feeding?" they asked.

As they pondered these questions, one morning Janardhana peered out of the kitchen window and saw a crowd gathered outside the building.

"Akshaya Patra *hai hai*," they chanted, holding up placards.

"Let the first vehicle come out of the kitchen — we will set fire to it," they said to the media.

The local politician had convinced them that their jobs were in danger. But this was not true.

"We have faced this issue before and we have a solution for it," assured Chanchalapathi from the head office.

The women involved in cooking would be retained by Akshaya Patra to receive food, serve food, clean the vessels and return them safely. And they would get the exact same salary.

"But they refuse to listen…" said Janardhana. "We will keep trying."

The Bhilai kitchen weathered the storm for several months. Finally, the elections took place. The mischief-monger lost his seat, as well as his deposit.

Raman Singh became Chief Minister for a second term. This time, he personally inaugurated the kitchen. After a delay of 18 months.

Around the same time, CM Y Rajashekhar Reddy invited Akshaya Patra to start a kitchen in Hyderabad. Things moved very quickly in this case.

"The CM has given orders to give the clearance by evening," said Chanchalapathi after the meeting. Within a month, Akshaya Patra was feeding 30,000 children.

A strong CM can move mountains in minutes. This was most evident in Gujarat, where Narendra Modi not only inaugurated the kitchen, he spoke about it in the Gujarat assembly.

"Aap log is program ko ek bada success story banaiye," Modi directed his bureaucrats.

In other states, the government provided land and free electricity. In Gujarat, they went a step further. Thinking out-of-the box.

The Chief Secretary spoke to three state PSUs: Gujarat State Fertiliser Corporation, Gujarat Industries Power Corporation, and Gujarat Alkalis and Chemicals. These PSUs supported the capital cost of building the Vadodara kitchen. As well as the recurring expenditure of feeding 1.4 lakh children.

Modi remarked, *"NGOs ke aane se mid-day meal program mein jaan aa jaati hai."*

The late Prime Minister Rajiv Gandhi once remarked that if the government spends one rupee on poverty alleviation, only 15 paise actually reaches the poor. This is due to leaks and lacunae in the system.

The mid-day meal scheme targeting 120 crore beneficiaries was no different.

Providing more nutrition to *netas* and *babus* than to schoolchildren.

CHAPTER 21

TAANDAV

"Every day we take so much rice — children just cannot eat it!"
This observation came from every kitchen Akshaya Patra
operated. As per government notification, children up to Class
5 were to get 100 grams of rice per day.

"Only Chhota Bheem will have such a big appetite!" said
the supervisors.

Consequently, Akshaya Patra decided to take a smaller
quantity of rice from the government. 70 grams per child
was more than sufficient. But the administration had their
difficulties with this.

"Sir, we are asking for less rice, not more," said
Chanchalapathi. "Why should there be any objection?"

It was an open secret that the amount of rice being
disbursed was in excess of what was needed. But these norms
had been fixed by the central government and everyone was

enjoying the bonanza.

Akshaya Patra presented its case to the state as well as to the Centre. Providing hard data to prove its claims. But they refused to budge.

"We cannot change the rules for one organisation," said one officer. "You please take the rice due to you."

Matters came to a head when the Centre sent a circular to the state education department asking why Karnataka was not consuming the amount of rice allotted towards the mid-day meal scheme.

Akshaya Patra had no choice but to accept tons of excess food grains. But silos in both kitchens in Bangalore were full to the point of overflowing.

"We will need to rent a godown somewhere to store this rice," said Chanchalapathi.

With all due permissions and paperwork, such a godown was procured.

But the actions of Akshaya Patra had not gone unnoticed. It was time to teach these do-gooders a lesson....

It was another busy day at Akshaya Patra's 16 kitchens across India. But in Bangalore, Chanchalapathi was staring at the television screen in dismay.

'Rice scam in Bangalore ISKCON temple?' read the NDTV news ticker. The reporter was interviewing two men holding sacks of rice.

"I have purchased rice from Akshaya Patra for ₹10," they claimed.

Such an absurd accusation. But there it was, flashing on the screen over and over again.

"You tell a lie enough times and a few people start believing it is true!" muttered Madhu Pandit darkly.

Indeed, Akshaya Patra received 13 tons of rice from the government every day. But the stock was meticulously accounted for.

"You can inspect our godowns anytime you want," he said to the press.

Yet the allegations continued.

'Akshaya Patra is misusing government grants!'

'These people are raising money by projecting India's poverty.'

In July 2009, the Karnataka government set up a House Committee to conduct a probe into the matter. A dark cloud hung over Akshaya Patra.

"The trustees are all firmly with us … but donors are asking questions," said Shridhar. The flow of funds was badly affected. So was morale.

Nevertheless, the show simply had to go on.

"Truth is on our side," said Chanchalapathi to his temple presidents. "We have nothing to fear."

But the weight of rumours was a heavy burden, on the monks, as well as the patrons. At the board meeting held in March 2010, all the trustees were agitated.

"Fingers are being pointed even at Mr Narayana Murthy,"

said Ramadas with great anguish. For the Infosys Foundation
was by then Akshaya Patra's single largest donor.

There was a great deal of anger, frustration and a feeling
of helplessness. There was pin-drop silence as finance director
Ramaswamy made his presentation.

The ninth slide read: '₹8 crore receivables from the
Karnataka government.'

In this climate of uncertainty, no state official wanted to be
caught 'helping' Akshaya Patra.

Mohan's face grew red and his voice angry. He turned
towards Madhu Pandit.

"Swamiji, enough is enough! Let's stop feeding. Then they
will know the value of Akshaya Patra!"

Ramadas, Abhay and Bala concurred.

"I agree. We should suspend the mid-day meal program in
Karnataka," said Desh. "At least for a few days."

All eyes were now on Madhu Pandit.

The monk took a deep breath and uttered one simple
statement.

"Hungry stomachs cannot shout."

If the feeding program stopped, the ones who would be
affected the most were the 5 lakh schoolchildren who had come
to depend upon Akshaya Patra.

Siva Sudhir watched in awe as the atmosphere in the room
quickly cooled down.

The trustees put on their thinking caps and chalked out a
new strategy.

"We have all the *challans*, certificates, facts and figures to prove our case," said Chanchalapathi. In fact, he had been trying to meet the Commissioner of Public Instruction to present Akshaya Patra's case. But with little success.

"Mr Kamath, if you call, we may get an appointment," suggested Chanchalapathi.

Abhay offered to speak to his various political contacts. In the following months, each did what he could for Akshaya Patra, even at the cost of his reputation. This included physically testifying before the House Committee.

Ramaswamy helped navigate the convoluted state government machinery. Procuring every possible certificate with stamp, seal and signature.

"Make sure supplies to the kitchen continue," he said to his assistant Siva Sudhir.

The young CA managed to convince hard-nosed vendors to keep the faith. He went on to make a sterling contribution which would have a lasting impact on the organisation.

The ICAI (Institute for Chartered Accountants in India) conducts an annual competition, the 'ICAI Awards for Excellence in Financial Reporting'. The award honours the select few who have gone the extra mile in their financial reporting requirements.

"Akshaya Patra must win the Gold Shield in this competition!" declared Siva Sudhir.

Working night and day, he put together an annual report that met the highest possible standard. When results were declared, Akshaya Patra won gold.

It was a moment of pride for the entire organisation. And a

big boost to its credibility.

During this 18-month ordeal, another supporter came to their rescue. Ravindra Chamaria took it upon himself to raise ₹5 crore. This time, Akshaya Patra would not need to take a loan to feed the children.

In February 2011, Akshaya Patra was exonerated of all charges. After thorough investigation, the House Committee presented its report to the Karnataka Legislative Assembly.

It concluded: 'There is no evidence to show the foundation misused funds meant for the program.'

Thus ended a trial by fire, with Akshaya Patra unsinged.

A building with strong foundations will stand tall and strong. So it is with reputation.

It is an asset which is not seen on the balance sheet.
But it is always with you and it travels everywhere.

Attracting the resources you need from halfway across the world.

CHAPTER 22

KUBERA

Bill Clinton stepped out of Air Force One at the seaside town of Port-au-Prince. But not for a vacation. The former President was visiting Haiti as a Special Envoy of the United Nations.

"I am here to help you rebuild your country," said Clinton. A year ago, Haiti had been struck by a devastating hurricane. There were no jobs and no food. The country was heavily dependent on humanitarian aid.

Clinton was accompanied by a business delegation. Among them, was Desh Deshpande.

The first stop on the two-day tour was a school in Cité Soleil, Haiti's largest slum. The highlight was the free mid-day meal to children, funded by the World Bank and local aid agencies.

"This is wonderful work," remarked the former President. The aid partner, 'Yele Haiti', had committed to serving 14,000 meals in schools as part of the Clinton Global Initiative.

As they walked back to the car, Desh remarked to Clinton, "Mr President, you must come to India and see the Akshaya Patra program. We feed 1 million children every day."

Clinton could not believe his ears: *1 million hot meals? How did they manage it?*

"You must visit us in India and see for yourself," said Desh. "I've pledged to help Akshaya Patra feed another 100,000 children in the next three years."

A promise that would not be forgotten.

The light of Akshaya Patra was spreading across the New World.

The CEO of Akshaya Patra scanned the roomful of people gathered at the Westin Hotel in Waltham, Massachusetts.

"The event is completely sold out," a member of the staff had just confirmed.

Over 500 attendees — doctors and engineers, journalists and entrepreneurs — had paid $140 each to attend the Boston fundraiser. As she climbed onto the stage, Madhu Sridhar recalled the initial days of Akshaya Patra USA when she had made presentations to small groups in their drawing rooms.

"We have come such a long way!" she thought to herself.

In a short span of three years, Madhu had created a solid grassroots organisation. With several local chapters and a strong donor base.

As always, the CEO of Akshaya Patra told the inspiring story of an organisation that started feeding 1,500 children, and scaled up to 1 million in the short span of 10 years.

"This has been possible due to many innovations and home-grown technologies."

By the time the video of the hi-tech Akshaya Patra kitchen had been played, the attendees were floored. Madhu ended her talk with an emotional appeal to the largely *desi* audience.

"All of us received subsidised education in India, that's why we are standing here. It is time to give back."

Keynote speaker Deepak Chopra then took the stage. He spoke about something everyone seeks but very few find: 'happiness'.

"Many Americans seek happiness from shopping," he said. "But the fastest way to feel happy is to make someone else happy."

That evening there were a lot of happy people in the room. Collectively, they raised over $400,000 for Akshaya Patra — enough to feed 28,000 children for a year.

At the end of the event, Deepak Chopra wrote out a cheque to Akshaya Patra. He was taken aback when the CEO of Akshaya Patra said to him, "Deepak, I want something more!"

Madhu wanted a commitment from the wellness guru to speak at an Akshaya Patra event once a year. Without charging a speaker fee. It was a request Deepak Chopra could not refuse.

When Nitin Nohria was named as Dean of Harvard Business School, Madhu sought a meeting with him. Dr Nohria spoke passionately about his childhood days when he lived in a remote village.

"I used to walk five miles to go to a better school — I know the value of a good education!"

He agreed to become a patron and evangelist for the program. Along with Narayana Murthy, Fareed Zakaria and Deepak Chopra, Nitin Nohria became part of the advisory board.

Their presence and influence helped raise the profile of Akshaya Patra USA.

At the heart of it all was the idea that anyone can make a difference. For a donation of just $14 ensured a hot mid-day meal for a child, for an entire year.

But donors were encouraged to make annual commitments. Or, go a step further.

"It is good to adopt a child but even better to adopt a school," said Dipika Khaitan, Executive Director of Akshaya Patra in the UK.

The question was how to make this happen. It was the support of Morari Bapu, India's most loved *kathakaar* that spread the message to a whole new audience.

Ravindra Chamaria was acquainted with Bapu and persuaded him to conduct an event in aid of Akshaya Patra.

"Main is sanstha ki paavan pravrutti se parichit hoon…" said Bapu to a packed audience at the Excel Centre in London. (I am familiar with the noble work of this organisation). In fact, he had seen it with his own eyes during a visit to the Vrindavan kitchen.

Being an authority on the *Ramacharitmanas*, Bapu talked about a philosophical dilemma that donors often face. Like the monkey prince Angad, who once questioned the practice of *annadaan*.

Morari Bapu clarified, "*Bhookhe ko anna dena daan nahi, apna kartavya hai.*" (To give food to the hungry is not charity, it is our duty).

Bapu's many followers in the NRI community were deeply inspired by his words. They came forward to donate £2,500 a year to feed the children of an entire school.

Donors could select a school in Gujarat, Rajasthan or Uttar Pradesh. Akshaya Patra would provide updates from the adopted school throughout the year.

"When you visit India, we will be happy to arrange for you to visit the school and the kitchen."

In this way, 150 schools were adopted, bringing meals to over 30,000 children.

The most creative ways to raise money, however, came from young people. The children of immigrants, who felt deeply for their counterparts in India.

A group of high school students in Michigan raised $30,000 through a variety entertainment show.

A teen performing her *arangetram* asked for donations to Akshaya Patra, instead of gifts.

In Texas, a girl fasted for an entire day. To know 'what hunger feels like'.

Money was thus raised, along with consciousness.

The most powerful number in the universe is 'one'. Each one can make a difference.

To spread this message, you need a medium. A town crier, a storyteller, a Narada *muni*. You need the travelling salesman of the modern age — the worldwide web.

CHAPTER 23

NARADA

"The internet is the future! You must start raising funds online!"

The year was 2010 and the comment took Chanchalapathi by surprise. For at that time, e-commerce was hardly known in India.

The suggestion came from Naveen Krishna Dasa, well-wisher of ISKCON Bangalore and a highly respected devotee (one of Prabhupada's original disciples).

Chanchalapathi was always open to new ideas.

"Can you find someone to start this new activity?" he asked Shridhar.

After a long and fruitless search, Ajay Kavishwar's name came up.

Ajay had left a promising job with Tejas Networks to work full-time at the temple five years back. From operating lifts to collecting change at the reception — no job was too small for him. He was now handling the sale of ISKCON merchandise.

When approached, Ajay said, "Prabhu, I do not know anything about internet marketing. But I am willing to try!"

For Ajay felt a deep and personal connection with the philosophy of Akshaya Patra.

As a child, he had been supported by an individual who had contributed ₹500 to his education. This enabled him to complete Class 10 from Vidya Vardhak Sangha High School and then become an electronics engineer.

From his very first salary, Ajay had started contributing ₹500 per month to Akshaya Patra. Now, it was time to raise the bar.

When you need a crash course in internet marketing, what do you do? Turn to the internet, of course. Ajay went a step further.

"If I have to learn, I must learn from the best!" he thought.

His research had thrown up the name 'Kevin Wilke', author of the 'Blue Pill/Red Pill' emailer which held the record for being opened by 100% of its recipients. Kevin Wilke ran a company called Nitro Marketing.

He picked up the phone and dialled the man's office.

"I am calling from India. I want to learn email marketing from Kevin," said Ajay.

Call it the assurance of youth or the audacity of hope, the

arrow found its mark.

"We have a division which mentors people," came the reply. "We will consider your request."

When Ajay revealed that he was representing a charity that feeds hungry children, Nitro Marketing agreed to suspend its $5,000 training fee.

"You can start the course now and pay us later," they said.

In a few weeks' time, Ajay was no longer a 'newbie'. He had learnt the basics of the internet and of writing good copy.

"It is very important to have a good subject line," said Ajay to his boss Shridhar.

Accordingly, his first email campaign to existing donors was crafted cleverly.

"Are you ashamed or proud to be Indian?" it said. The mail was opened by many, and generated some donations. This boosted Ajay's confidence.

While the message was well-crafted, there was no way to spread it far and wide. For advertising costs money and Akshaya Patra worked on 'zero budget'.

It was then that Ajay stumbled upon Google grants, a scheme under which non-profits could receive up to $10,000 per month for Adwords.

To apply for the grant, one had to submit sample ad copy. There are various rules that one must follow, including the number of characters per line.

Ajay and his wife searched Google for hours and learnt all they could about how to write a great Google ad.

But even as he kept hoping and praying for the grant, Ajay

focused his energies on another neglected area — the Akshaya Patra website. The site was simply a PowerPoint presentation which had been uploaded online. It yielded barely ₹2,000– ₹5,000 in donations per month.

Ajay located an expert, Ram Anand, to overhaul the website.

"I commit 100 hours of my time to you free of cost," said Ram.

By the time the Google grant was approved, Akshaya Patra had a spanking new website with an Internet Payment Gateway and PayPal payment option.

The first donation came from Hong Kong. It was a sum of ₹5 lakh.

When Ajay received a call from his colleague he could not believe his ears.

"Are you counting the zeroes properly?" he asked. "Please ask this person if he really wants to donate ₹5 lakh … or is it a mistake!"

It was no mistake; the donation was from the CEO of Merrill Lynch in Hong Kong.

While Ajay was convinced about the power of the internet, others in the organisation were unsure. The question was how to make the best use of limited resources.

As an employee of ISKCON, Ajay had been managing the sale of merchandise which generated ₹1 crore in revenue per month. Much of this came to Akshaya Patra in the form of donations.

Whereas, after all efforts, online marketing was bringing in only ₹3–4 lakh per month.

"Let us close it down," said Shridhar at one meeting.

But Ajay was not one to give up so easily. He took Shridhar to meet Dr Mani Shiva Subramanian. A paediatric surgeon who was also a successful internet marketer.

Dr Mani treated children with congenital heart disease free of cost. But he raised money for their hospital costs through his website. He was a mentor to Ajay.

Dr Mani said, "Every new idea has a gestation period. If you believe in this idea, then be patient for three to five years. Only then will you reap the benefits."

These words convinced the CEO of Akshaya Patra to back Ajay's efforts.

Meanwhile, Ajay was determined to show results. Inspired by Kevin Wilke, he set a target which 'would not let him sleep at night'.

And he achieved that target of raising ₹1 crore in the very first year.

Around this time, ISKCON volunteer Saanil Bhaskaran had accepted the challenge of setting up a telemarketing team for Akshaya Patra. He had taken a sabbatical from his high-paying consulting job in order to do this.

Akshaya Patra had been working with an external agency, with little to show for it.

"We need to start our own call centres," said Saanil. This would require an investment of ₹25 lakh. Ravindra Chamaria stepped forward in support.

The Akshaya Patra call centre started as a small office just outside the temple premises, employing 30 people. Most of them were women from poor families.

Employees were given three weeks of training and a week of mock calls. In a year's time, this too showed good results.

In 2011, Ajay and Saanil joined hands to do something completely out of the box.

"All I want to do is learn search marketing from the best in the world," said Ajay.

He had reached out to the foremost expert in the field, Gillian Mussig, also known as 'SEO Mom'. She was keen to visit India and help Akshaya Patra pro-bono.

"But we need to take care of her airfare."

That's when the duo came up with a brilliant idea.

"There must be many who want to learn from Gillian Mussig. Let us organise a conference and charge the participants a small fee of ₹2,000."

In March 2011, a Search Marketing conference was organised at the ISKCON temple. It was attended by 200 people, including a contingent from Germany.

Speakers who were used to 5-star hotels and fancy cars stayed at the modest ISKCON guesthouse and were driven around in TATA Indicas.

"We will use Akshaya Patra as a case study," decided Ajay. The experts ripped apart every aspect of the NGO's online strategy, from the colour scheme of the website to the SEO optimisation.

The Akshaya Patra team hung on to every word and furiously took notes.

At the end of the year, Ajay and Saanil organised another, equally ambitious event. The purpose this time was to learn everything about social media marketing.

The 'Social India' conference featured seven international and five Indian speakers. It was another resounding success.

"Akshaya Patra is trending on Twitter!" exclaimed Ajay with glee.

We tend to celebrate success and to hide failure. But they are two sides of the very same coin.

While success makes one arrogant, failure keeps you humble.

Humility is a good teacher, a faithful companion. As you walk the long and winding road towards your goal.

CHAPTER 24

VIJAYA

"*Cyclewale bhaiya aa gaye!*"

Schoolchildren gathered around as *bhaiyya* opened his *dabba*. Quickly he doled out the day's lunch: *chhole* in *haldi* water, with half-cooked, lumpy rice.

"*Khatam ho gaya!*" he announced within minutes. Half the children were still in queue, holding their plates.

This was the 'mid-day meal' in India's capital city. Brazenly flouting the norms laid down by the Honourable Supreme Court.

It was under these circumstances that Delhi Chief Minister Sheila Dixit invited Akshaya Patra to start a kitchen.

"I want you to feed 2.5 lakh children," she declared at the first meeting.

"All we need is some land; we are ready to start!" said Chanchalapathi.

The Akshaya Patra team was keen to start in the capital. For no matter how much good work it was doing in Karnataka or Rajasthan or Orissa, it would never come to the notice of *mantris* and *babus* at the highest level.

"You do remember what happened last time," remarked Mohan.

Back in 2004, in the very early days of its expansion, Akshaya Patra had tried, and failed, to start operations in Delhi.

Despite the support of Sunil Mittal of Bharti Enterprises, there were vested interests and tangled threads of bureaucracy which had made it impossible to function.

"That was many years ago," said Chanchalapathi. "Now we are much wiser. We will find a way."

It was the eternal optimist speaking. Little did he know what obstacles lay ahead....

In other states, government land or buildings had been allotted by the CM. But in Delhi, things were different.

"You must meet the Lieutenant Governor — land matters are under him," advised a well-wisher. So, they paid him a visit.

The Lt. Governor was encouraging. But even though both DDA (Delhi Development Authority) and MCD (Municipal Corporation of Delhi) were under him, he said, "Land is expensive in Delhi. It is difficult to spare."

So Akshaya Patra decided to set up a kitchen on its own steam.

"Let us rent a building and convert it into a kitchen," said Madhu Pandit.

Now came the matter of permissions. Luckily, the education department fell under the Chief Minister. So Akshaya Patra was confident — *kaam ho jayega.*

The CM took the application and made some calls. But it remained stuck.

Finally, she threw up her hands and said, "You should understand Delhi…"

The wheels within wheels, the sleaze and the grease. Contractors started approaching Akshaya Patra.

"Hamare paas license hai. Kitne bachche chahiye — ek lakh, do lakh, paanch lakh?"

All they wanted was '75 paise' per child. The mid-day meal was an organised racket. Take ₹2.50 from the government and provide a meal worth not more than ₹1. Pocket the difference and make handsome profits.

"The number of children they claim to feed is more than the number enrolled!"

Real money was collected by contractors for 'ghost' children.

Nevertheless, Akshaya Patra stood its ground. Finally, without any bribes, they secured permission to feed 30,000 children for three months.

But it was not the end of their problems. Getting rice from the government was a herculean task. And collecting the subsidy per child was a nightmare!

"Prabhu, we are working in nine other states, nowhere do we run around in circles like this!" said Chanchalapathi in anguish one morning.

In every other state, the headmaster submitted the attendance sheet to the Block Education Officer and the District Magistrate released the funds.

In Delhi, the money was remitted to the headmaster. Akshaya Patra therefore had to visit each school; 150 schools meant 150 headmasters.

The last straw was the unrealistic menu set by the government. All other kitchens managed within a cost per meal of ₹7. But the Delhi government insisted that puris be served to the children, and the cost had shot up to ₹17!

"This is food fit for a wedding party, not for schools!" said the cooks, as they sweated over *kadaais*.

This was an unhealthy situation — for the children and for Akshaya Patra.

A decision was taken to close down the kitchen. One year later, dues of ₹46 lakh remained 'pending' from the Delhi Government.

This was one time that Akshaya Patra failed spectacularly. But soon, it would celebrate a spectacular success.

Back in the year 2008, Akshaya Patra had set an audacious goal: to serve 1 billion meals by the end of 2011.

At the function where this announcement was made, Infosys Chairman N R Narayana Murthy shared a memorable story.

"I used to survive by eating just a chocolate bar a day on the last week of every month when I was working in Paris in the 1970s," he shared.

On those days, he would quietly disappear from the lunchroom.

"In fact, such starvation affected my memory to an extent," he noted.

No child must sit in a classroom with an empty stomach. This idea powered the Akshaya Patra team to grow faster and aim higher.

The goal of 1 billion meals was achieved in September 2012. The song composed by Shankar Mahadevan on the occasion said it all.

Hamein likhna hai, padhna hai, aage hi badhna hai
Khaate hain yeh kasam,
Paao shiksha, paao bhojan
Swasth man ho, swasth jeevan.

But what was the impact of these 1 billion meals?

"Let us speak to some children who have completed their schooling," said Shridhar.

Some days later, a young man walked into the Akshaya Patra office. He was carrying a white envelope in his hand.

"My name is Darshan," he said. "I am the son of a security guard."

Darshan's father had an income of ₹1,500 per month and six mouths to feed. There was never enough to eat. The government school provided free education, but Darshan often fainted in class and had no interest in studies. Then, Akshaya Patra came to his school.

That one meal a day changed his life.

"I started working hard. My marks improved from 40 to 60, 60 to 80!"

In Class 10, Darshan scored 92% and received a ₹5,000 scholarship from Akshaya Patra. He went on to do a BTech in Computer Science, first class with distinction.

"Sir, this is my offer letter from HCL Technologies," he said shyly.

The boy who could barely pass his exams was now an engineer earning ₹20,000.

A phone with 10% battery cannot last the day. So it is with a hungry child.

The mid-day meal is a charger. Infusing energy into the body, accelerating the mind.

CHAPTER 25

VYAVASTHA

There was a festive air at the Raajkiya Madhyamik Sanskrit Vidyalaya in Pratapnagar, Jaipur.

"Amrika ke pradhan mantri hamare school mein aa rahe hain," the children whispered gleefully, as they waited to welcome their visitor in traditional Indian style.

Clinton arrived at 10.40 am, accompanied by a 25-strong delegation. He spent the next 30 minutes interacting with students and serving them the mid-day meal.

At the end of the visit he concluded, "This is a remarkable partnership!"

For nowhere in the world were the government, the business community and an NGO working together — to serve 1.3 million children each day.

And yet, Akshaya Patra covered barely 1% of India's 120 million school-going children. The majority of mid-day meals

rested on the tired shoulders of headmasters and teachers.

"*Kya hum khana banayenge ya bachchon ko padhayenge?*" they wondered. Meals thus prepared were often inadequate. And occasionally, dangerous.

In July 2013, tragedy struck at a primary school in Saran district of Bihar when 23 students died after consuming a mid-day meal. The food was found to be contaminated with pesticides.

In the aftermath, Akshaya Patra was called in as the official training partner for the national mid-day meal program. Programs on food safety and personal hygiene were conducted for cooks, helpers and block education officers. Participants were provided with a kit comprising an apron, towels, gloves, soap, nail cutter, cap and utensil holders.

"We want to ensure that such incidents never recur," said the government of Bihar.

But was Akshaya Patra immune to accidents? It was a question that often troubled Chanchalapathi.

For a single case of food poisoning could destroy the credibility built over 15 years....

The mid-day meal was halfway done when one of the teachers came running into the courtyard and screamed, "*Khaane mein chhipkali hai!*" (There is a lizard in the food).

The children, who had been happily eating *dal-chawal* a

minute ago, suddenly started feeling sick. They were rushed to the district hospital to have their stomachs pumped.

All eyes turned to the Akshaya Patra kitchen in Jaipur, which had supplied the meal.

"Our kitchen is ISO 22000 — let us track which batch of dal went to this school," said Ratnangada Govinda. It was found that the same dal had been supplied to 40 other schools, without incident.

When the lizard was sent for testing, the lab found that it was a *pahadi chhipkali* — a species not seen in urban areas. Therefore, it was concluded that the lizard fell into the vessel at the school itself.

But some months later, there was another incident; this time in Bangalore. Once again, Akshaya Patra got a clean chit, but the management was worried.

Around the same time, the Jamsetji Tata Trust came forward with a donation of ₹55 crore.

"We would like to use this money to improve our food safety standards," said Chanchalapathi.

The Tata Trust agreed to cover the cost of hiring qualified food safety inspectors in all 23 mid-day meal kitchens. In addition, Akshaya Patra would set up a modern food safety laboratory in four cities: Ahmedabad, Lucknow, Bangalore and Bhubaneswar.

Meanwhile, due to a government mandate, all listed companies had to devote 2% of their profit to CSR activity. The Infosys Foundation was flush with funds.

"We commit ₹127 crore to Akshaya Patra over the next 5 years," they said.

This would mainly be used to build and operate three modern kitchens — in Jodhpur, Hyderabad and Mysore. Bringing 200,000 more children into the Akshaya Patra fold.

"We must keep building systems and processes," said Shridhar. Even that .001% chance of a slip-up would have to be eliminated.

This could only be done by a qualified professional.

Muralidhar Pundla had worked with the quality department at large tech companies like Flextronics and Motorola. But when he was approached by his former boss to work for Akshaya Patra, he said 'yes' without hesitation.

Murali was already associated with ISKCON as a devotee.

"This is not a job for me, it is something much more," he said.

To Murali's trained eye, Akshaya Patra was not a 'kitchen', but a high-volume manufacturing facility.

The new General Manager (Process Excellence) was about to bring new ideas to everyone in the organisation — from the PhDs to the *matajis* cutting vegetables.

"Our training modules must be in local languages and use a lot of visuals," Murali said to his team.

Every little aspect, from the washing of rice, to sanitising the knife and cutting board, was explained to workers in this manner. And it improved efficiency as well as morale.

"Sir, now I have understood why and I will do same thing at home also," said the women.

A training period of 40 hours was made mandatory — at the time of induction as well as on the job.

Steps were taken to improve the storage of raw material, with labels and expiry dates written in large lettering. But the most important new development was the introduction of kaizen.

'Kai' means change and 'Zen' means good, so, loosely, this Japanese management practice means 'change for the better'. And it happens through small, continuous improvements.

"I believe that each one of us can make a difference," Murali said to his staff and supervisors.

Every Akshaya Patra worker — cook, driver, helper or cleaner — was encouraged to share ideas and suggestions for improvement.

In the Bangalore kitchen, there was a suggestion that rice be cooked with starch instead of draining it. By using this method, the kitchen was able to save 6,000 litres of water.

"The preparation time for one batch of rice has come down by four minutes!" said a delighted Vinay Kumar, Head of Operations.

A CA by training, Vinay once worked with a company that sold ERP systems to SMEs. He came to Akshaya Patra on a sales call, and decided to join the organisation.

Unlike Murali, Vinay was not a follower of ISKCON. But he was impressed by the work of Akshaya Patra and the chance to serve the cause of children.

"You don't have anyone to implement the ERP solution — I will help you do it."

This entailed travelling to every Akshaya Patra location across India. By the end of the project, Vinay knew the workings of the kitchen in and out.

Until 2012, every Akshaya Patra kitchen was headed by an ISKCON monk. Some of them expressed the desire to be relieved of this duty. Thus Vinay became the first professional to assume responsibility for kitchen operations in Bangalore, Bellary, Vrindavan and Lucknow. With unit managers reporting to him from each centre.

Now, it was time for Murali to work his magic. He introduced the managerial and supervisory staff to the concept of 'Six Sigma'.

"Companies like Motorola and GE have used this technique — so can we!" he said.

Under Murali's guidance, Akshaya Patra trained 100 'green belts' in Six Sigma. These champions worked to identify and implement projects at various kitchens. One of the most successful was 'route optimisation', using Google map coordinates. The Vrindavan kitchen was able to reduce travel time and drop two vehicles from its rosters.

"Over 5,000 kaizens and 22 Six Sigma projects have saved Akshaya Patra ₹1.8 crore," said a beaming Chanchalapathi at the annual board meeting.

Both Murali and Vinay felt a glow of inner satisfaction. The salary at Akshaya Patra was modest, but the 'bonus' was priceless.

Human existence is the search for meaning. This search takes some to the Himalayas. But one need not go that far.

Working for a cause is like a spiritual Six Sigma project. It heals you, it changes you. It raises the bar.

CHAPTER 26

VIVEKA

On 25 April 2015, at 11.56 am, Nepal was struck by a devastating earthquake.

Three days later, Akshaya Patra received a communication from the Prime Minister's office.

"There is acute food shortage — Nepal needs urgent assistance!"

By the next morning, Akshaya Patra had prepared 100,000 meals which were transported to Delhi and airlifted to Nepal. The Akshaya Patra team then met the Principal Secretary, National Disaster Management Authority (NDMA) to prepare a Plan of Action.

"We must quickly set up an open kitchen facility in Nepal," they said.

The Tata Trust came forward to fund the infrastructure while the Nepali NGO Sipradian Sahayata Sanstha provided ground assistance. The challenge before Akshaya Patra was how to set up operations in the shortest possible time.

"We can divert some of the cauldrons and boilers ordered for the Lucknow kitchen," said R Madan, COO of Akshaya Patra.

Madan had recently joined from PepsiCo — a man bubbling with ideas and in a hurry to implement them. Just the man to handle a crisis like this one.

Cauldrons, boilers and food grains were transported by road from Bangalore, Pune, Lucknow and Valsad to Bhaktapur in Nepal. The last equipment arrived on 14 June.

Five days later, the 2,500 square foot kitchen was up and running. The first 1,000 meals were served on 19 June.

Over the next 88 days, the Akshaya Patra Earthquake Relief Centralised Kitchen served over 1.4 million meals to 17 camps in and around Bhaktapur.

On 21 September, the kitchen was handed over to the local partner Sipradian Sahayata Sanstha. Who was now trained and equipped to handle it.

"We are happy to share our know-how with any organisation," said Chanchalapathi.

But never did Akshaya Patra sit back and say 'we know it all'. There is always a better way to do things. Seek and ye shall find....

It was a bitterly cold December morning when Jaganmohan and Madan arrived in the city of Lund, in Sweden.

"Wow, what a factory!" exclaimed Madan as they entered

the Tetra Pak plant.

Established in 1951 by entrepreneur Ruben Rausing, the company is best-known for inventing the 'tetra pak carton' which we use every day.

What few know is that Tetra Pak is also the world leader in cutting-edge, completely automated food-processing machines.

"I am excited to see the Albatch system," said Jaganmohan, with childlike enthusiasm.

The Tetra Albatch™ is a processing system for the batch production of food. And Madan believed it was faster and cheaper than cooking in cauldrons.

"We will be able to cook 800 kgs of rice in 25 minutes!" said Madan when he put forth the idea. Eight times faster than the current technology in use.

The beauty of Albatch was that it required no mixing or stirring. Just input the ingredients and the system gave you the finished product.

However, the Albatch machine was used to make ketchup and chocolate syrup. The only Indian company using the technology was Dabur, for Chyawanprash.

"Can the machine make tasty sambar, rice and sabzi?" asked Chanchalapathi.

That's what the Akshaya Patra team had come to Sweden to find out.

The Tetra Pak engineers input the Indian dal, rice, spices and vegetables that had arrived from India in a shipping container. Jaganmohan and Madan waited with bated breath for the first batch to roll out.

On tasting the first spoonful of sambar, their eyes lit up. *"Ekdum* perfect!" exclaimed Jaganmohan.

The trials went on for three days with batches of bisi bele bhath, lemon rice, pulao and khichdi. The results were fantastic.

"Dil maange more!" said a group of Indian software engineers completing a project on-site. They were happy to have such tasty Indian food in a foreign land.

Finally, Chanchalapathi arrived in Sweden to sign on the dotted line. After much negotiation, Akshaya Patra placed an order for six Albatch machines.

These machines would be installed in the new kitchens, starting from Hyderabad.

But some months later, Madan left Akshaya Patra. With his exit, the project lost steam. And there were many doubts.

The cost of each machine was ₹6 crore. On top of that, the government was unwilling to waive custom duty.

"We are promoting 'Make in India' — can you not make this machine locally?" the Principal Secretary asked.

Finally, Chanchalapathi and Shridhar decided to buy one machine, to honour the commitment made. And to see its impact on kitchen operations.

"If we really do save a lot of money, then it is worth buying more," they thought.

The question was: is big really better? For at the same time, another idea had found a champion within the organisation. The idea that 'small is beautiful'.

In 2012, Akshaya Patra had won the Marico Innovation

Award. As a result, Akshaya Patra had received mentoring from an organisation called Innovation Alchemy.

"We want to help you do something you think is not possible," they said.

At the Billionth Meal celebrations, Narayana Murthy had remarked that Akshaya Patra should also start giving children breakfast.

It was a noble thought but very difficult to implement.

Vinay Kumar was the man deputed by Akshaya Patra to work with Innovation Alchemy. Vinay and his team put every aspect of the kitchen under the scanner.

"The first batch of rice is cooked at 5.30 am and eaten at noon," they noted. This was inevitable in the centralised kitchen model.

The innovation that emerged was the 'hub and spoke model'.

The centralised kitchen would act as the 'hub' and do the pre-preparation work. Ingredients would be delivered to a smaller kitchen called the 'spoke'. This kitchen would have a capacity of 25,000 meals and deliver in a 15-km radius.

"The meals will be hot and more fresh!" said Vinay, explaining the model to Shridhar. It would even be possible to introduce breakfast.

With fewer kilometres to cover, the vehicle could deliver *naashta* and make a second trip with lunch.

"With less meals to cook, we can begin work at 6 am instead of 4 am," added Vinay. This would make it easier to retain workers.

The biggest selling point was that a spoke kitchen could be set up at a lower cost.

"We can look for donors willing to give lakhs instead of crores!"

Shridhar was convinced about the merits of the hub and spoke model and pushed for it internally. But the various department heads were not convinced.

The project went into hibernation. Until a worrying directive was issued by the HRD ministry to all its mid-day meal partners.

It said: 'Mid-day meals must not be cooked more than 20 km from the schools'.

A directive is more like 'advice' than a binding order. Hence it did not affect the existing operations of Akshaya Patra. But what about the future?

"Rules keep changing," said Chanchalapathi. "We should not be caught by surprise."

The hub and spoke model thus got a new lease of life. The idea is now being implemented in Vrindavan, where schools are spread far and wide.

It takes courage to let several flowers bloom in the same garden. But such a garden is more beautiful, more bountiful.

The gardener must watch over the seedlings. And weed out what does not work.

CHAPTER 27

BHAVISHYA

"*Aajkal saade saat sau rupaye mein kya milta hai?*" asks actor
Ranveer Singh. (What can you buy in ₹750?)

Two tickets to a multiplex? One drink at the bar? If you go
to a branded clothing shop, you won't even get a handkerchief.

*What you can get in ₹750 is a mid-day meal for a child — for
the entire year!*

This was the 'India Ke Hunger Ki Bajao' campaign run
by Ching's Secret, Yashraj Films and Reliance Fresh, to raise
money for Akshaya Patra.

This was how Damodar Mall found himself at the Hubli
mid-day meal kitchen. The CEO of Reliance Fresh was
fascinated by scale.

"I must see for myself how they make 100,000 hot Indian
meals a day!"

Damodar Mall was mighty impressed by the entire

operation.

This could be a factory of Nestle or Hindustan Unilever....
It's a world-class facility!

By 7 am, the cooking was done. Vans were loaded with large, stainless steel tiffins carrying sambar and rice. Then off they went to deliver their hot lunches.

By 8 am, there was a lull in the activity. Workers started leaving.

"*Ab kya hoga kitchen mein?*" he asked the Operations Manager.

"We will clean the kitchen and start preparations for the next day at 7 pm."

Damodar Mall was stunned. No profit-making organisation would leave its factory idle for half the day. There was 50% spare capacity at the Akshaya Patra kitchen.

And, slowly, an idea started forming in Damodar Mall's market-driven brain.

Idli and dosa batter were outselling instant noodles at all his stores. In the near future, customers would like to pick up hot, freshly-cooked food as well.

And what better place to source such meals from than the Akshaya Patra kitchen?

What's more, Reliance would add a profit margin and a 'CSR margin' to each meal.

Every meal sold would thus subsidise an Akshaya Patra meal for a child.

But there was just one doubt in Damodar Mall's mind: "Would a non-profit be willing to work for-profit by selling its meals?"

Unknown to him, this was a path Akshaya Patra itself had embarked on.

In May 2014, an entity by the name of Akshaya Nidhi had been registered.

After much debate and discussion, the trustees had been convinced to let Akshaya Patra go 'commercial'.

"There is demand from industrial establishments for our food," said Vinay. "If we sell to them, we can generate income."

All profit would, of course, be donated to Akshaya Patra.

Thus Akshaya Patra began supplying meals to several construction sites in Gurgaon and to factories in Bangalore. The meals were supplied at ₹25 per plate.

The feedback was very positive, both from the labourers and their bosses.

"Our Gurgaon site is the only one with 0% attrition," said a senior manager at DLF.

A private school in Bangalore started subscribing to the Akshaya Patra meal as well.

In its first year of operation, Akshaya Nidhi earned ₹9 crore and donated ₹1 crore in profits to the mother organisation.

So when Damodar Mall approached Shridhar, he was open to the idea.

The Reliance Fresh team worked with the Akshaya Patra team to devise a standardised product with adequate shelf life. Idli and dosa batter are now prepared in the mid-day meal kitchen after the day's lunch is dispatched. The product is available in Reliance Fresh stores in Bangalore.

Damodar Mall has bigger plans for this revolutionary project.

"Hot sabzi, roti and dal from Akshaya Patra will sell from my stores someday."

Beyond kindness and goodness, Akshaya Patra can become a part of your life. Like buying Amul Butter — because you love it.

An act of consumerism, which benefits the farmers. But you don't even realise it.

In May 2016, Akshaya Patra received the Nikkei Asia prize for 'Economic and Business Innovation'. At the awards ceremony in Tokyo, Madhu Pandit reflected on the journey so far.

"I remember the day the first meal was served ... the children loved the food but never expected that we would come with food the next day too."

They did go the next day. And the next. And never has a meal been skipped in the last 16 years. In fact, a total of 2 billion meals have now been served!

On 27 August 2016, the holy precincts of the ISKCON Radha Krishna temple bore a festive air. For it was time to celebrate this journey, this milestone.

Here I am to bow down…
Here I am to worship…

The sweet strains of the invocation song by the St Joseph's Convent Girls' High School choir (Frazer Town) set the tone for the evening.

On the dais were the President of India, the Chief Minister of Karnataka, the Governor of Karnataka, the Union HRD minister and a galaxy of well wishers. For the story of Akshaya Patra is a unique one, where hundreds of strangers gathered together — often mysteriously — for a selfless cause.

Serving 13,800 schools across 11 states, today, Akshaya Patra is the largest program of its kind in the world.

"Yet, every day in the morning, we are humbled because there is more to do!" said Mohandas Pai.

The dream is to reach 5 million children by the year 2020.

"We pray to God … that he gives us the strength every single day!"

The strength to have compassion, to have commitment. To think of the 'other' as one of our own.

Like the 'akshaya patra' granted by Krishna to Draupadi, may the modern Akshaya Patra be that inexhaustible vessel.

For no child should be hungry in India. No child should be hungry in this world.

Vasudhaiva Kutumbakam.

ADDENDUM

Mohandas Pai is now Chairman of the Manipal Global Education Group and remains a passionate evangelist for Akshaya Patra.

V Balakrishnan has left Infosys and joined the Aam Aadmi Party. He remains on the Akshaya Patra board.

Emily Rosenbaum is now CEO of Akshaya Patra USA. Bhawani Singh Shekhawat is the CEO of Akshaya Patra UK.

Rishi Sunak, son-in-law of Sudha Murty, was elected to the British Parliament in May 2015. He fondly remembers the meal at Akshaya Patra as the best meal he has ever had in India.

R Madan and Chitranga Chaitanya Dasa are no longer with Akshaya Patra.

Vikram Krishna remains an ISKCON devotee but lives in the US, where he works for McKinsey & Co.

Suvyakta Narasimha Dasa is now working on a dream project of ISKCON in Vrindavan called the 'Chandrodaya mandir', which, when completed, will be the tallest temple in the world.

Siva Sudhir, the CA who helped Akshaya Patra win the ICAI gold medal, left Akshaya Patra to become an ISKCON monk. He is now known as Shyama Vallabha Dasa.

Twice unlucky, Akshaya Patra is attempting to start a kitchen in Delhi a third time. This time, supported by CM Arvind Kejriwal.

Four new kitchens are coming up in Uttar Pradesh with a feeding capacity of 100,000 each. The UP government is bearing the capital cost of these kitchens.

In August 2016, Akshaya Patra made its first foray in Maharashtra, starting a feeding program in Nagpur.

Akshaya Vidya — inspired by Dr Abdul Kalam — was shut down after three years. So that Akshaya Patra could focus all its attention on the mid-day meal.

The latest impact study conducted in eight states across India showed impressively high attendance rates (above 90%) in schools that get Akshaya Patra meals.

Akshaya Patra currently serves 1.5 million meals every day from 24 locations across 11 states.

In the matter of ISKCON Bangalore vs. ISKCON Mumbai, the trial court has ruled in favour of ISKCON Bangalore. However, appeals in the higher courts continue.

Despite this ongoing battle, Akshaya Patra opened its kitchen to ISKCON Mumbai for inspection. To help them start their own school mid-day meal program called Annamrita 'Food for Life'.

The total number of mid-day meals served in India each day is 120 crore, across 12.65 lakh schools. Most of them receive sub-standard meals.

What if the Akshaya Patra model was adopted and implemented across the nation?

Feeding a child is not charity, it is our collective duty. Let us do it well.

EPILOGUE

I Am That.
I Am the Sun, the Stars, the Stones.
I Am the Breath, the Flesh, the Bones.
I Am the Sorrow, the Anger, the Pain
I Am the Plant, the Fruit, the Grain
I Am the Thought, the Word, the Deed.
I Am the Hungry Mouth that you Feed.
I Am Nothing and Nothing I Do.
You are but Me and I am but You.

AKSHAYA PATRA KITCHENS

27 locations in 11 states (as of July 2016)

Centralised kitchens:

June 2000 — Bangalore (H K Hill)

August 2003 — Vrindavan

February 2004 — Jaipur

July 2004 — Bellary

August 2004 — Mangalore

December 2004 — Hubli

June 2006 — Bangalore (V K Hill)

June 2006 — Puri

June 2006 — Nathdwara

July 2007 — Mysore

October 2008 — Hyderabad

October 2008 — Vishakhapatnam

January 2009 — Bhilai

November 2009 — Baroda

February 2010 — Guwahati

July 2011 — Chennai

June 2012 — Surat

August 2013 — Jodhpur

November 2013 — Rourkela

July 2014 — Cuttack

August 2014 — Ahmedabad
March 2015 — Lucknow
November 2015 — Vijaywada
December 2015 — Kakinada
August 2016 — Nagpur

Decentralised kitchens:

April 2005 — Baran
March 2007 — Nayagarh

HOW YOU CAN CONTRIBUTE

It takes ₹950 to feed a child for a year!
https://www.akshayapatra.org/onlinedonations
(Every donation of ₹500 or above is eligible for 100% tax
exemption under Section 35AC or 50% tax exemption under
Section 80G of the Indian Income Tax)

Other donations:
   Sponsor kitchen equipment
   Donate a vehicle
   Sponsor a school for a year

Also consider:
   Donate in memory of a loved one
   Donate on the occasion of (a birthday, wedding
   or anniversary)
   Donate in honour of (anyone you wish)

(I personally request any school, college, corporate or charity
which invites me NOT to gift me mementos, flowers, shawl,
pen or any knick-knacks. Instead, please donate the money
you have budgeted for this to Akshaya Patra.)

THANK YOU!

During the course of our research we heard about and spoke to many more individuals who shared their insights, their stories. Although all the material could not be included in the book, we would like to acknowledge their contribution to Akshaya Patra.

Monks who built and managed kitchens:
1. Satya Gaura Chandra Dasa & Lakshmikanta Dasa: Hyderabad
2. Stoka Krishna Dasa, Jai Chaitanya Dasa & Mahaprabhu Gauranga Dasa: Mysore
3. Karunya Sagar Dasa: Mangalore
4. Niskinchana Bhakta Dasa: Vishakapatnam
5. Radhakanta Dasa: logistics and facilities
6. Nandanandan Dasa: projects and infrastructure

Well-wishers of Akshaya Patra:
1. Ranjan Pai: Chairman, Manipal Group
2. Lalit Panwar: IAS officer
3. Harin Thaker: chairman of Akshaya Patra UK
4. B V Jagadeesh: serial tech entrepreneur and director at Akshaya Patra USA.
5. Jaishree Deshpande: philanthropist
6. Salone Mittal Ghosh: development consultant
7. Ramanan Raghavendran: founder, Impact Partners

Professionals who continue to grow Akshaya Patra:

8. Emily Rosenbaum: CEO, Akshaya Patra USA
9. Bhawani Singh Shekhawat: CEO, Akshaya Patra UK
10. Vandana Tilak: Advisory Board Member, Akshaya Patra USA
11. Bhavin Raval: Food Safety Lab manager, Ahmedabad

Public leaders who have supported Akshaya Patra:

1. Atal Bihari Vajpayee: former PM of India
2. Dr Manmohan Singh: former PM of India
3. Tarun Gogoi: former CM of Assam
4. Dr Himanta Biswa Sarma: Health minister, Assam
5. Kum. Mayawati: former CM of Uttar Pradesh
6. Akhilesh Yadav: current CM of Uttar Pradesh
7. N Dharam Singh: 17th CM of Karnataka
8. H D Kumaraswamy: 18th CM of Karnataka
9. B S Yeddyurappa: 19th CM of Karnataka
10. Siddaramaiah: current CM of Karnataka
11. Ashok Gehlot: former CM of Rajasthan
12. Chandrababu Naidu: current CM of Andhra Pradesh
13. K Chandrasekhar Rao: first and current CM of Telangana
14. Anandiben Patel: former CM of Gujarat
15. Vijay Rupani: current CM of Gujarat